THE DUMB INVESTOR

HOW THE EVERYDAY INVESTOR CAN BEAT THE PROS

Ankur Bansal

COPYRIGHT AND DISCLAIMER

A QUICK WORD BEFORE WE START

Look, I'm a guy sharing what I've learned over thirty years in the trenches. I'm not your broker, I'm not your CPA, and I don't know your personal life. Think of this book as a map I drew for myself—not a "command" for you to follow. Investing is a risk, and the market can be a beast. If you're going to bet your life savings, talk to a licensed pro who knows your specific situation first.

LEGAL DISCLAIMER & COPYRIGHT

No Professional Advice
The content of this book is for **educational and informational purposes only** and does not constitute

investment, financial, tax, or legal advice. The author is not a licensed financial advisor. Nothing in this book should be interpreted as a recommendation to buy, sell, or hold any security, fund, or other financial product.

Risk of Loss

Investing and trading involve significant **risk, including the loss of principal**. Past performance **is not indicative of future results**; there is no guarantee that any strategy mentioned will achieve its objectives. Examples and illustrations are hypothetical or based on historical data and are **not guarantees of future performance**. Readers must consider their own financial goals and risk tolerance. Consulting a **qualified professional** is strongly recommended.

Disclaimer of Warranty

Information is provided **"as-is."** While the author believes the data and citations (including S&P 500®, U.S. Treasury, and other sources) are accurate, the author and Vernon Hills Consulting LLC assume no responsibility for errors, omissions, or any loss or damage resulting from the use of the information contained herein.

Trademark Acknowledgments

- **S&P 500®, SPDR®, and S&P CoreLogic Case-Shiller®** are registered trademarks of S&P Dow Jones Indices LLC.
- **Apple® and iPhone®** are registered trademarks of Apple Inc.
- All other trademarks, service marks, and logos used in this book are the property of their respective owners.

PREFACE

I have been an active investor for most of my life. My journey began in a college dorm room in the late 1990s, at the very dawn of the digital age. It was a time when, for the first time in history, a world of information was suddenly available at our fingertips thanks to the internet and the rise of search engines like Google.

I used this newfound freedom to teach myself everything I could about the markets. I spent my time diving into the mechanics of various asset classes, learning how stock markets actually move, and trying to make sense of dense financial statements. I began following investing legends like **Warren Buffett**, **Benjamin Graham**, and **Peter Lynch**, convinced that if I could learn their craft, I would make myself a lot of money.

Which I did.

The "aha!" moment came in 2016–17 when I was buying shares of Apple, only to realize that Warren Buffett—the man I had spent half a lifetime trying to **emulate**—was doing the exact same thing. It was the ultimate validation. In my mind, it was the definitive proof that I had finally "cracked the Buffett code" and mastered the complex craft of the legends.

Or at least, that's what I thought.

But soon enough, I realized the stock markets themselves were on a remarkable run, and I couldn't be certain if my "expertise" was actually doing anything special to move the needle. I truly loved the hard work I had put in during my investment journey—the research, the spreadsheets, and the thrill of the chase. But the more I looked at the results, the more I arrived at the one hard-won lesson of my thirty years in the arena:

In the markets, "more effort" rarely equals "more wealth."

Leonardo da Vinci once said that **simplicity is the ultimate sophistication.** Nowhere is this truer than in the world of investment. A handful of clear principles and a steady hand are almost always more effective than an army of Ivy League analysts and their proprietary algorithms.

But the modern financial industry has built a wall around this simple truth.

They've taken a straightforward journey and buried it under layers of jargon and "premium" services. They want you to believe that success requires a complex guide—and a hefty fee—when in reality, the most sophisticated move you can make is to simply get out of your own way.

This book is a rejection of that complexity.

In 1949, Benjamin Graham—the mentor to Warren Buffett—published *The Intelligent Investor*. Buffett famously called it "by far the best book on investing ever written." I couldn't agree more. Graham's book is a masterpiece of rigorous, technical mastery, written for those willing to spend a lifetime mastering the craft.

But let's be honest: This book is not that book.

The Dumb Investor takes the opposite approach. I've written it for those who recognize that in an over-complicated world, **simplicity is the winning edge.** This book is for the person who is smart enough to want the results of the market but wise enough to know their time is better spent elsewhere.

Whether you consider yourself a "**dummy**" at finance or you are simply a high-achiever who refuses to trade your life's precious hours for cluttered trading screens, this book is for you.

My goal isn't to turn you into an investment expert. Instead, we are going to focus on a handful of simple, guiding principles—the kind that ensure your investment journey is successful while you continue doing what you love. We are going to stop trying to outsmart the market and start **out-simplifying** it.

Welcome to the smartness of "Dumb Money."

TABLE OF CONTENTS

INTRODUCTION

Investing is very old! We've been trying to make our money work for us for as long as we've been around. The tools and methods have changed—but the goal is the same: we want the stuff we have today to be worth more tomorrow. While the way we invest has evolved, the spirit of the thing is pretty much the same. At its heart, it's about **harnessing the collective progress of society**, allowing you to benefit from the fruits of everyone's labor, not just your own.

When people bought shares of Coca-Cola in 1920 or Apple in 1984, they weren't just betting on a soda or a computer. Not really. They were betting on the whole American system. They were counting on the fact that the roads would stay paved, the schools would keep turning out smart kids, and the police would keep the peace. You were betting that the "**American Dream**" wasn't just a slogan—it was a functioning machine.

But it goes deeper than that. These companies didn't just win because of America; they won because the rest of the world stayed mostly sane. They needed global markets to buy their stuff and scientists in other countries to keep moving tech forward. It's a fundamental reality: you can't have a massive payday if the world is on fire. **Prosperity** and **conflict** just don't hang out in the same room.

In today's world, we're drowning in information. You can Google anything, fall down a YouTube rabbit hole, or listen to a dozen books on your phone. If you want to learn to code or bake a simple cake, the path is clear: you follow the recipe, you practice, and you get better. Most skills follow a simple rule: more effort usually means more progress.

But investing? Investing is a different animal.

It's the only skill I've found where you can do all the '**homework**," follow every rule, and still wake up poorer than you were yesterday. I'm sure there are other hard things in life, but nothing else seems to take your hard work and throw it back in your face quite like the markets. It's a journey that isn't a straight line; it's a rollercoaster.

INVESTING MEANS SOMETHING DIFFERENT TO EVERYONE

You've got a massive menu of places to put your money—stocks, real estate, gold, or even just a basic savings account. Every one of them plays by a different set of rules, and most people naturally stick to what they already understand.

But here's the kicker: even after you pick your spot, the hard part is just starting. You're still stuck with the big questions: ***How much? When? For how long?*** The truth is, there is no **"manual"** for this—at least none that I've ever found. To make matters worse, if you ask five different financial advisors for the "**right**" answer, you'll probably get six different opinions. Half the time, they don't even speak the same language.

Investing isn't a science where you can just flip to the back of the book and find the answer. It's **messy**, it's **abstract**, and at the end of the day, it's **deeply personal**.

THE MARKET NEVER SITS STILL

The market is a moving target. It's constantly being pushed around by messy politics, wars, new technology, and a million other things we can't control.

But if you want to know who is really pulling the strings, you have to look at **interest rates**.

Think of the Federal Reserve—**the "Fed,"** which is just the central bank of the United States—as the guy with his hand on the economy's thermostat. [1] When things get too "hot"—meaning prices are rising too fast and inflation is out of control—the Fed raises interest rates to cool things down. They did this in 2022, and it wasn't pretty. It made borrowing money more expensive for everyone. When it costs more for a company to get a loan or for you to get a mortgage, people spend less. And when spending drops, the price of everything—from houses to groceries—eventually starts to cool off.

But there's a catch. If the Fed cools things down too much, businesses stop making money and people start losing jobs. That's a recession. Once that happens, the Fed usually panics and lowers rates again to **"spark"** the engine.

This back-and-forth—the Fed turning the heat up and then cranking it back down—is the heartbeat of the whole system. As an investor, you're stuck right in the middle of it.

You can see this whole cycle in action in the diagram right here.[2]

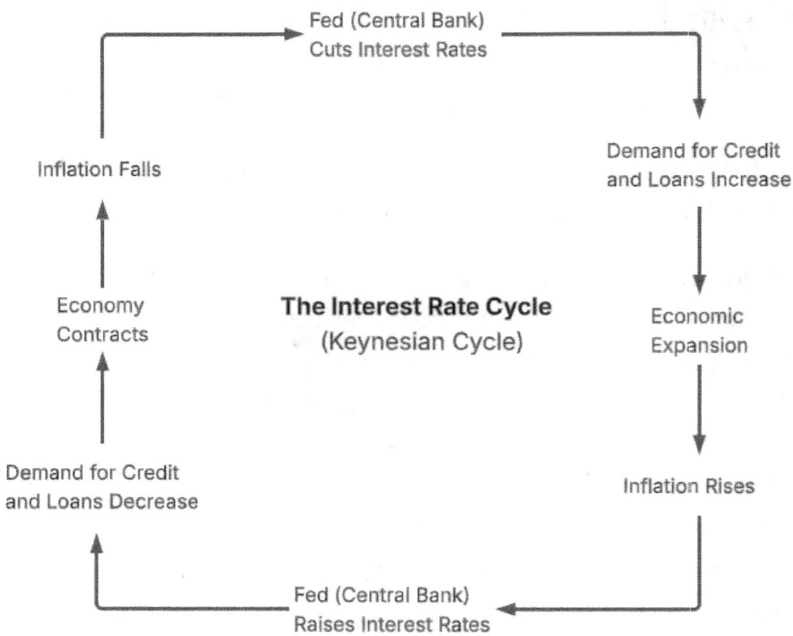

Note: A quick nod to the experts: This diagram is based on the legendary 1936 work by John Maynard Keynes (often called *The General Theory*).[3] It's the classic way to show how central banks try to keep the economy from either overheating or freezing over.

THE RULES AND THE EXCEPTIONS

Generally speaking, rising rates are bad news for stocks, real estate, and bonds. They make your savings account look a lot better, but they put a squeeze on almost everything else. Predicting where these rates are going is a nightmare—even the "**experts**" with the expensive suits get it wrong all the time. I've learned not to trust anyone who claims they can do it consistently.

But here's the thing: the **"Interest Rate Cycle"** I just showed you is the textbook version. In the real world, the economy gets messy.

Sometimes you get **Stagflation**—which is a fancy word for a total disaster where prices keep going up even though the economy is standing still. Or you get a **Liquidity Trap**, where the Fed lowers rates but nobody feels like spending a dime. These are the outliers that remind us that the market isn't a machine—it's a living, breathing thing that doesn't always follow the map.

Then there's the big one: Oil.

Oil is the lifeblood of the system. When it gets expensive, everything else gets expensive, and the Fed is forced to hike rates to stop the bleeding. We saw this back in the **'70s**—oil prices went through the roof, inflation followed, and the whole world ended up in a recession.

We're moving toward green energy now, but don't think that means the drama is over. We're just trading our old oil addiction for **Energy Metals** like copper, lithium, and nickel.

In my view, these materials could become the "**new oil**"—the essential lifeblood of every battery and electric car on the planet. As the world leans on them more, they're going to bring their own brand of chaos to the markets.

STOCKS: THE MOVING TARGET

Of all the places you can put your money, **stocks** are usually the main event because, historically, that's where the real growth has always happened. But here's the catch: when you buy a stock, you're buying a living, breathing business. And businesses are under constant attack.

A company that looks invincible today can be gone tomorrow if they don't keep up. Look at the old giants like **Sears** or **Toys "R" Us**. They were the kings of the world until e-commerce came along and wiped them off the map. They didn't see the wave coming until they were already underwater.

This is why I say investing is so hard to master. You aren't just learning a set of rules and then going home. You're trying to hit a moving target while the wind is blowing and the target itself is changing shape. It never stops evolving, and it doesn't care about your "homework."

INVESTING IS AN EMOTIONAL BOXING MATCH

You'll hear all sorts of theories about what investing actually is. Some people will tell you it's a **math problem** that requires a supercomputer. Others think it's a **trend-spotting game** where you just have to follow the right crowd.

But from where I'm sitting, they're both wrong—or at least that's how it looks to me. Investing isn't about numbers or trends—it's an **emotional boxing match**. And the two biggest heavyweights in the ring? **Greed** and **Fear**.

When the market is booming, greed starts whispering in your ear to bet the house. When it crashes, fear screams at you to sell everything and run. The more time you spend staring at the ticker, the more these emotions start to take over your brain.

Even some of the smartest people in history have been knocked out by this. Take **Sir Isaac Newton**. The man literally discovered gravity, yet he lost a fortune in the "South Sea Bubble." Afterward, he famously said:

> **I can calculate the motion of heavenly bodies, but not the madness of people.**[4]

If a genius like Newton couldn't handle the madness, what hope do the rest of us have?

It's not about having a "stratospheric IQ." As Warren Buffett says, you don't need to be a genius to win at this. You just need a solid plan and the guts to keep your emotions from "**corroding**" that plan. In his words:

> **To invest successfully over a lifetime does not require a stratospheric IQ, unusual business insights, or inside information. What's needed is a sound intellectual framework for making decisions and the ability to keep emotions from corroding that framework. You must supply the emotional discipline.**[5]

At the end of the day, your biggest enemy in investing isn't the market—it's the person you see in the mirror.

INVESTING IS JUST A BET ON TOMORROW

Every time you put your money into a stock or a property, you're making a prediction. You can call it "**research**" or "**due diligence**" to make yourself feel better, but at the end of the day, you're placing a bet. You're betting that what you're buying today will be worth more tomorrow.

You're basically trying to look into the future with a **cloudy crystal ball**. You use your knowledge and your analysis to try and see what's coming, but the truth is, the future doesn't owe you anything. I've learned that the hard way.

Success is never guaranteed, no matter how many hours of "homework" you do. I've always loved how the physicist Niels Bohr put it:

> **Prediction is very difficult, especially if it's about the future.**[6]

This is the hardest part for people to swallow. You can be the smartest person in the room and do the best analysis on earth, and you can still get wiped out because the future is a **moving target**. It's not that your math was wrong. It's just that the world changed while you were busy calculating.

WHAT TO EXPECT FROM THIS BOOK

I wrote this book to turn the "**less is more**" philosophy into something you can actually use—a **strategy that runs on autopilot** while you're out living your life. We're moving away from the stress of checking tickers every ten minutes and moving toward a system that stays in the background, exactly where it belongs.

In the pages ahead, we're going to strip away the jargon and get down to the few steps that actually matter. Here is the "Dumb Investor" promise for the portfolio we're building:

- **Beating the "Pros":** We aren't looking for miracles, but this system is designed to capture market growth and, more often than not, leave the high-priced fund managers in the dust over the long haul.
- **Getting Your Weekends Back**: This is built for simplicity—the kind I try to follow in my own investing. I want you to spend less time looking at spreadsheets and more time doing literally anything else.
- **The Sleep-Well Factor:** We will explore a highly personalized asset allocation strategy that provides absolute clarity on your financial health.

The most important thing to remember is that our goal is to **remain dummies.** You're not going to walk out of this book as a Wall Street expert—and that's a good thing. You'll walk away with a **few guiding principles** that keep your money growing while you focus on your work, your hobbies, and your family.

We're going to look at today's market, figure out which asset classes actually deserve your hard-earned cash, and build a portfolio that has stood the test of time. I'm not asking you to take my word for it. I'm going to show you exactly why this works

---

A Quick Reminder: Before we move on, remember that this book is my personal map—not a direct command for your bank account. The examples and portfolios I show you are here to teach you how the market works, but the market doesn't follow a script. Investing always involves risk. Please check out the full legal disclaimer at the beginning of the book for the "official" details before you start moving your money around.

CHAPTER 1
WHAT IS INVESTING

If you want to understand the difference between a real investor and someone just throwing darts at a board, you have to go back to the source. Benjamin Graham—the legend who shaped Warren Buffett's entire approach to building wealth—drew a very clear line in the sand:

> **An investment operation is one which, upon thorough analysis, promises safety of principal and an adequate return. Operations not meeting these requirements are speculative.**[7]

In plain English? If you haven't done the work to make sure your money is safe, you're not investing—you're gambling, plain and simple.

Now, Graham uses the word **"promise."** In today's world, we know there are no 100% guarantees, but that doesn't mean we should be reckless. To me, that "promise" is about the effort you put in **before** you click **buy**.

To survive and thrive in the high-stakes arena of investing, you need two things: a Playbook and a Rulebook.

I've boiled the **Playbook** down to what I call the **4 Qs of Investing**. These are the four big moves you have to make to gain ground. But moves alone won't save you if you ignore the **Rulebook**. That's where the **Dumb Investor's Commandments** come in—the core principles that act as your guardrails, keeping you from doing something stupid when the market gets crazy.

THE 4Qs: THE ONLY FOUR MOVES THAT MATTER

I've seen a lot of people lose a lot of money, and usually, it's because they skipped the basics. You shouldn't put a single dollar into the market until you've answered four critical questions. This isn't just "homework"—it's your survival guide.

Q1: WHERE SHOULD I INVEST

This is everyone's favorite part. It's the "**hot tip**" you hear at a wedding or the "**life-changing**" stock your brother-in-law won't stop talking about over coffee. It's easy to get swept up in the hype. But let's be honest: buying a stock because someone "**pitched**" it to you isn't investing. It's shooting in the dark and praying you hit the bull's-eye. Luck is great when it happens, but "**hope**" is a terrible strategy for your retirement.

Take the EV (Electric Vehicle) craze. Everyone is hunting for the **next Tesla stock** to ride to the moon. But do you actually understand how the car business works? Do you know the **nuts and bolts** of the industry—the razor-thin margins and the battery supply chains—or are you just buying a cool story?

I see it all the time: people will spend three weeks researching which $800 smartphone to buy—checking every review and comparing every camera spec. Then, they'll turn around and drop $8,000 on a stock they heard about in a 30-second TikTok video. **It's madness.**

If you want to win, you have to stay within your **"Circle of Competence."** If you've spent twenty years in real estate, you probably know a bargain when you see one. If you're a doctor, you likely understand medical tech better than any Wall Street analyst. Use that unfair advantage.

In other words: If you don't understand the business, don't buy the stock. It's okay to say "I don't know" to 99% of the market as long as you are 100% sure about the 1% you actually buy.

As Warren Buffett famously said:

> **Know your circle of competence, and stick within it. The size of that circle is not very important; knowing its boundaries, however, is vital.**[8]

Q2: WHEN SHOULD I INVEST? (STOP CHASING THE SHINY OBJECT)

Most people think "**when**" is simply the moment they figure out a hot stock. They hear a tip at a BBQ, see a "game-changer" headline, or finally connect the dots on a new trend and think, ***"This is it—I have to get in right now."*** But more often, that "when" is just driven by **impulse**.

We get so caught up in the "story" that we ignore the price tag altogether. We don't stop to ask if the company is actually worth the money; we just ask, ***"How do I get my piece before the price goes higher?"***

As Warren Buffett famously warned:

> **You can turn any investment into a bad deal by paying too much.**[9]

Look at the poor souls who bought **Cisco Systems** in March 2000. It was the "hottest" thing on the planet—the literal backbone of the internet. Everyone had finally "figured out" that the web was the future. People weren't looking at the math; they were looking at the hype. They paid **$82 a share** because they were terrified of being left behind.

They were right about the company, but they were dead wrong about the price.

Cisco's business actually exploded over the next 26 years. Revenues shot up from $18.9 billion to $57.7 billion, and profits rose to $10.3 billion. It remained a dominant, world-class engine of the tech world.

But because those investors ignored the price tag in 2000, they had to wait nearly 26 years just to see their money again. They finally "**broke even**" in early February 2026, only to watch the stock dip again a few days later. Think about that: **over a quarter-century** of waiting, just to end up back where you started.

We don't do this as much with anything else. When you buy a house, you don't usually say, "I'll pay double what it's worth because I really like the kitchen!" You check the appraisal, you look at what the neighbors paid, and you walk away if the price is insane.

But in the stock market? When the price starts skyrocketing, people actually get more comfortable buying.

WHY THE BLIND SPOT?

Why are we so careful with a house but so reckless with a stock? It's because a house is simple. You can walk through the rooms, check the roof, and look at the "comps" on the same street. It's one building on one piece of dirt.

A company? That's a different beast. It's a massive machine with a thousand moving parts—employees, inventory, debt, and competitors trying to eat its lunch every day. Trying to figure out what all those pieces are actually worth is hard. Wall Street loves to throw around fancy terms like **Discounted Cash Flow** or **Enterprise Value** to make it sound like a science, but for most people, it's just overwhelming.

It's much easier to see that a company is "**great**" than it is to know if it's a "**bargain**." We see a line of people at the Apple store and think, **"This company is winning!"** That's easy. But knowing if the stock is worth $150 or $250? That's where we get into trouble.

And that's usually when people give up on the math and try to "**time**" the market instead—thinking they can buy at the absolute "**bottom**" and sell at the "**peak**" like they've got a crystal ball tucked in their desk.

Good luck with that.

The truth is, trying to time the market is a losing game. I've tried it myself—it's unpredictable, it's exhausting, and even the "experts" get it wrong half the time. Most people just end up panicking and selling at the worst possible moment.

As Ken Fisher famously put it:

> **Time in the market beats timing the market—almost always.**[10]

In other words: Stop trying to be a psychic. You don't need to guess where the market is going tomorrow. You just need to get in, stay in, and let time do the heavy lifting for you.

Q3: HOW MUCH SHOULD I INVEST

Have you ever kicked yourself for not betting more on a winner? I know I have—it's a sickening feeling. You do all the work, you find the right company, you buy it at the right price, and then—because you only put in a tiny amount—the profit doesn't even cover a nice dinner.

On the flip side, people often "bet the farm" on a hunch and lose everything.

Finding a "wonderful company" at a "wonderful price" (Q1 and Q2) is the foundation. Once you've done that homework, you have to decide how much of your hard-earned cash to actually commit. This isn't rocket science—it's about **weighting the probabilities.**

Think of it as evaluating the weight of the evidence. When the facts point to a near-certain winner, you increase your position. When the evidence is weak, you stay small or walk away. In the market, if a company checks all your boxes, the likelihood of success is higher. You don't have a crystal ball—nothing is ever guaranteed—but the size of your investment should match your level of conviction.

When the **probability** looks great, you can justify a bigger position. When the idea feels "average" or the story is a bit fuzzy, you stay small. You don't have to be a hero on every trade.

But there is one catch: **Liquidity.** Never invest money that you might need for next month's rent or an emergency car repair. There is nothing worse than being forced to sell a great investment at a loss—just because your water heater broke. Keep enough "boring" cash on the side so you never have to be a **forced seller** out of desperation.

Q4: HOW LONG SHOULD I INVEST (THE SELLING PROBLEM)

Most people ask "When should I sell?" before they've even finished buying. That's a mistake. The length of your **time horizon**—how long you're willing to stay in the seat—is actually your greatest superpower.

If you're looking for a quick buck in a year or two, you aren't investing; you're gambling. And the odds are ugly.

THE ROLLERCOASTER OF ONE YEAR

Aswath Damodaran—a guy often called the "Dean of Valuation" because he's spent decades crunching every number in market history—has some data that every investor needs to see. Looking at market returns from 1928 all the way to 2025, the numbers tell a brutal story about the short term.

Over any single year, the "big three"—stocks, real estate, and gold—are all over the place. One year you're up 30%, the next you're down 20%. If you need that money for a wedding or a down payment in twelve months, you are basically flipping a coin with your life savings.

The only thing that stays steady in the short term is the 3-month T-bill. It's boring, it's backed by the government, and it won't make you rich, but it also won't leave you broke when you need to pay the bills.

For the Dumb Investor, the rule is simple: If you can't commit to the seat for at least five years, stay away from the "hot" stuff. Time is the only thing that smooths out the bumps.

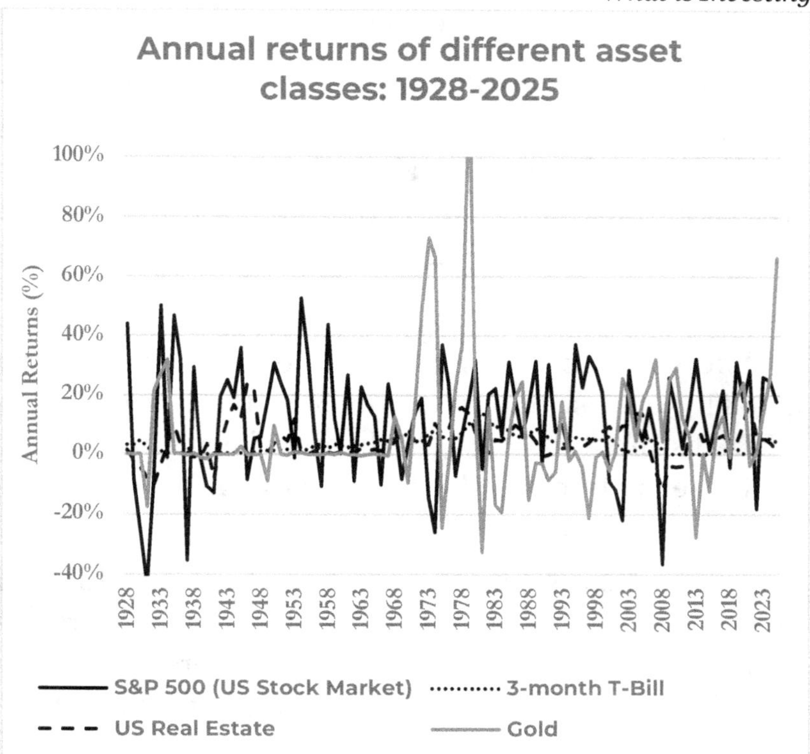

Source: Aswath Damodaran's Historical Market Data (1928-2025).[11]

A Quick Note on the Numbers:

- **The S&P 500®**: This is just a fancy name for a "bucket" of the 500 biggest companies in America. When I say "stocks" in this chapter, that's the bucket I'm talking about.

- **Negative Returns**: This is Wall Street's polite way of saying you lost money. If the chart shows -5%, it means your $100 just became $95. Ouch. Which is exactly why you don't take these risks with money you need for rent.

HOW TIME KILLS RISK

The table below shows the single most important secret in the market: **The longer you stay on the ride, the harder it is for the market to hurt you.** Even the "risky" stuff like stocks starts to look safe if you can just keep your hands off the steering wheel and let the engine run.

- **The One-Year Coin Flip:** Over a single year, the S&P 500 lost money 26 times in the last 98 years. That's more than a 25% chance of being in the red. Those are terrible odds if you're using that money for next year's rent.
- **The 15-Year Sure Thing:** Once you stretch that out to a 15-year window, the odds of losing money drop to 1 out of 6. And for Gold? Since 1928, there hasn't been a single 15-year period where it ended in the negative.

Time is the ultimate vacuum cleaner—it sucks the risk right out of the room. I've seen it work over and over in my own investing, and it never gets old.

CHANCES OF LOSING MONEY (1928 To 2025)				
Holding Period	**S&P 500**	**3-month T-Bill**	**U.S. Real Estate**	**Gold**
1 Year	26 out of 98	0 out of 98	15 out of 98	34 out of 98
5 years	3 out of 19	0 out of 19	1 out of 19	4 out of 19
10 years	2 out of 9	0 out of 9	1 out of 9	2 out of 9
15 years	1 out of 6	0 out of 6	1 out of 6	0 out of 6

Note: Data is based on non-overlapping "back-to-back" blocks of history from 1928 through 2025.

Source: Damodaran, Aswath. Historical Returns on Stocks, Bonds and Bills: 1928-2025[12]

KEY TAKEAWAYS

- **Short-term is a coin flip.** If you need the money in a year, don't put it in the market. Between the "big three" (stocks, real estate, and gold), you've got a massive chance of getting punched in the mouth.
- **Time is a vacuum cleaner.** The longer you **stay in your seat**, the more the risk gets sucked out of the room. At 15 years, the "scary" stuff starts looking like a sure thing.
- **Boring is safe.** T-bills won't make you a millionaire, but they are the only things that won't leave you broke when the water heater breaks.
- **Stop trying to be a psychic.** You can't control the market, but you can control your clock. The longer you wait, the more the math works for you instead of against you.

THE DUMB INVESTOR'S COMMANDMENTS

Having a great **Playbook** is how you move the ball, but the **Rulebook** is what keeps you in the market. You can have the most aggressive offensive plays in history, but if you ignore the rules, you'll be penalized until you're out of cash and out of capital.

Beyond the tactical moves and the math of the 4Qs, there are a few core principles—the **Commandments**—that govern the field. These aren't just polite suggestions; they are the hard constraints that keep your head on straight and stop your strategy from crashing when the market goes crazy.

COMMANDMENT #1: PROTECT THE PRINCIPAL

Your first priority isn't to get rich—it's to stay rich. Or at the very least, **don't get poor.**

Making "okay" returns is fine. But losing your principal—the actual cash you worked your tail off to save—is the ultimate sin. In the market, a bad return is a headache; losing your capital is a catastrophe. Warren Buffett, the greatest investor of all time, summed this up in two simple rules:

> **Rule No. 1: Never Lose Money. Rule No. 2: Never Forget Rule No. 1**[13]

HISTORY IS A GRAVEYARD OF "SURE THINGS"

Don't let anyone tell you an investment is "safe."

- **1929 and 2008:** Millions of people thought real estate and stocks were "safe" until their savings vaporized. [14]
- **Gold:** People treat gold like a security blanket, but it's dropped by 20% or more four times since 1928.[15] If you bought at the peak, you got burned.
- **Banks:** In the '30s, 9,000 banks simply vanished. Even "cash in the bank" wasn't a guarantee.

Even U.S. Treasuries—the closest thing we have to a "sure thing"—came hair-raisingly close to a default in 2011 because of a political shouting match in D.C.

The Lesson: Nothing is 100% safe.

THE "BURNED FINGER" TRAP

Most people play a losing game of **"Follow the Crowd."** They get scared and run to a savings account after a crash ("burning their fingers"), only to realize they're missing out when the market starts to roar again. So, they jump back in right at the top, just in time to get punched in the mouth again.

This isn't investing; it's chasing your tail. If you don't respect the risk from the start, you'll spend your whole life confused, broke, and angry at a chart.

DOING THE HOMEWORK

Now, let's be real. The future is a mess and nothing is a sure thing. You will see red numbers on your screen eventually. But there's a difference between a market dip and a total wipeout.

You protect your principal by doing your homework. I've learned the hard way that buying a stock just because someone on TV mentioned it is a fast track to regret—you take risks you actually understand. As Buffett puts it:

> **Risk comes from not knowing what you're doing.**[16]

If you don't understand the business, you're not really investing—you're gambling with the lights off. The Dumb Investor stays safe by only playing in the backyard they know—really know.

COMMANDMENT #2: DEMAND AN ADEQUATE RETURN

People love a good fairy tale, especially when it involves money. If someone offers you a "guaranteed" 20% annual return, you should check your pockets and walk away. Why? Because in the real world, that's not an investment—it's a fantasy.

We fall for these claims because we're human. I've fallen for a few myself. But I want to show you the difference between "Doing Great" and "Living in a Dream World."

THE 25-YEAR REALITY CHECK

Imagine you started in 1998. You put away $100 every single year for 25 years. Let's look at three different paths your money could have taken:

- **The "Market" (S&P 500)**: You just bought the 500 biggest companies in America and sat on your hands.[17]
- **The "GOAT" (Berkshire Hathaway)**: You gave your money to Warren Buffett—the greatest investor to ever live.
- **The "Magic Beans" (20% return):** You found that "guaranteed" investment someone was pitching.

The results by the end of 2022? A real wake-up call:

- **The S&P 500** (including dividends) grew at 8.64%. Your money became $436,190. (That is a massive win!)
- Berkshire Hathaway grew at 9.82%. Your money became **$525,030**. (Even better.)
- The "**Magic Beans**" would have hit $2,831,886.

Look at that gap. If the greatest investor in history "only" got you to half a million, why do you think a random pitchman can get you to nearly three million?

The Lesson: When you chase 20%, you aren't just being "ambitious"—you're being reckless. Chasing unrealistic returns is the fastest way to break Commandment #1 and lose your principal.

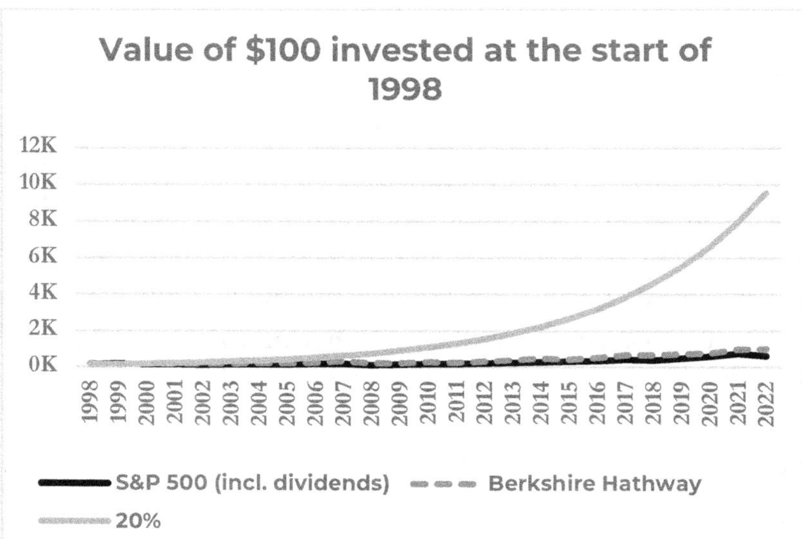

Source: Damodaran, Aswath (S&P 500); Macrotrends (Berkshire Hathaway).[18]

Since 1928, the S&P 500 has averaged about **10.02%** (with dividends reinvested). That is your benchmark. Anything significantly higher than that isn't an "opportunity"; it's a red flag.

COMMANDMENT #3: CASH IS YOUR OXYGEN

You can have the best investment strategy in the world, but if you don't have cash in your pocket when your car's transmission explodes, your plan is going to fail. In the market, **liquidity is oxygen.** If you run out of it, you stop breathing, and you're forced to do the one thing a Dumb Investor must never do: **Sell in a panic.**

THE "FORCED SELLER" PENALTY

When you break a term deposit early, the bank hits you with a penalty. But when you're forced to sell stocks or real estate because you're desperate for cash, the **market** hits you with its own penalty. The market smells desperation. If you have to sell during a downturn just to pay your mortgage, you aren't "investing" anymore—you're getting robbed. You're breaking **Commandment #1** and bleeding out your principal just to stay afloat.

THE RAINY-DAY BUFFER

This is why you never, ever invest every cent you own. You need an emergency fund—a pile of cash sitting in a boring, "liquid" savings account that you can grab in five minutes.

This fund isn't there to make you money—it's there to protect your investments. Think of it as the "moat" around your castle. When the roof leaks or the water heater dies, you go to the savings account, not your portfolio.

By keeping your **"living money"** separate from your **"market money,"** you ensure that even when life gets messy, your seat in the market stays occupied.

HOW MUCH OXYGEN DO YOU NEED?

Think of this as the final safety check for Q3 (How Much Should I Invest?). You can only afford to put a big bet on the table if your "Oxygen tank" is full enough to keep you breathing during a crash.

The standard advice is to keep three to six months of living expenses in your emergency fund.[19] I've seen plenty of people follow that blindly—and get burned. "Standard" doesn't account for your specific life. To a Dumb Investor, the answer is simple: **You need enough cash to ensure you never, ever have to touch your long-term "seat" in the market.**

To find your number, stop "reflecting" and start looking at the cold, hard facts of your life:

- **The "Bench" Time:** If you got fired tomorrow, how long would you be "on the bench"? If you're a specialized brain surgeon, you might find work in a week. If you're in a niche industry that's shrinking, you might be hunting for a year. **If your industry is shaky, your fund needs to be huge.**
- **The Leaky Tap:** Is your paycheck a steady stream (salary) or a leaky tap (commission/freelance)? If you don't know exactly what's hitting your bank account

next month, you need a 12-month "moat" to sleep at night.

- **The Deductible Nightmare:** Look at your insurance. If you have a $5,000 deductible on your health or car insurance, that money needs to be sitting in cash. If it's not, a single car accident will turn you into a "forced seller" in the market.
- **The Mouths You Feed:** If it's just you and a cat, you can be aggressive. If you have a spouse, three kids, and a mortgage, you are the "Single Point of Failure." The more people who rely on you, the bigger the safety net needs to be.

THE VERDICT. Most people settle for 3 months. For the Dumb Investor, 6 months is the sweet spot. It's the "sleep-well-at-night" number. Now, if you're young, single, and have a steady firehose of a salary, you might start with 3 months just to get your wheels turning (we'll see an example of this later with Mr. Dumb Money Manager). But as your life gets bigger, your moat needs to get deeper. Aim for 6.

WHAT IF THE TANK IS EMPTY?

If your "Oxygen tank" is empty, it's usually for one of four reasons. None of them are "wrong," but you need to be honest about which one you're dealing with:

- **You're at the Starting Line.** Building a safety net takes time. Don't beat yourself up for being a beginner—just keep filling the tank. Every $50 is another minute of "oxygen."

- **The Tank Did Its Job.** If your transmission exploded and you spent your savings to fix it—congratulations. You used the oxygen so you didn't have to drown in debt. Your only mission now is to stop "aggressive" investing and refill the tank.
- **The Leaky Lifestyle.** If you have a decent income but no savings, you have a "**hole in the bucket.**" This isn't about "reviewing budgets"; it's about being honest about your lifestyle. If you're spending your emergency fund on $12 cocktails or a new TV, you aren't "**unlucky**"—you're unprotected. You're trading your future security for a weekend of fun.
- **The Tiny Tap.** If your income is a drip, the habit is more important than the number. Saving your first **$100** is a massive win—it's the spark that starts the whole engine.

COMMANDMENT #4: LEVERAGE: THE CHAINSAW

In simple terms, leverage is just a fancy word for **betting with money you don't have.** It's borrowing funds to "amplify" your buying power. It's what you do when you buy a $200,000 house with a $40,000 down payment. You're using the bank's money to own an asset you couldn't afford on your own.

THE LESSON

Leverage is the most seductive tool in finance because it makes you feel like a genius when things are going up. If that $200,000 house goes up $10%, you haven't just made

$10%—you've nearly doubled your $40,000 investment. This is why the "Genius Investors" love it. They think they've found a shortcut to wealth.

But remember: **A chainsaw doesn't care if it's cutting wood or cutting your leg off.** When you leverage your life—whether it's through a mortgage or a margin account—you are trading safety for speed. If the market shifts just a few inches the wrong way, that "amplified" power turns into an amplified disaster.

THE VERDICT

To me, leverage is a necessary evil for a home, but a deadly poison for a portfolio. We don't use it to "get ahead" faster because we know that the faster you go, the harder you hit the wall. **If you can't afford to lose the money, don't borrow it to place a bet.**

THE CHAINSAW KICKS BACK

- **Market Risk.** A 15% drop in the housing market doesn't just mean a "notional loss." If you bought a $200,000 house with $40,000 down, and the price drops to $170,000, nearly **all of your equity is gone.** This is exactly what millions of families faced during the 2008 crash.

  But here's the reality check: your house doesn't know what it's "worth." Even if the market says the price is down, the roof still keeps the rain out, and your family still has a place to sleep. As long as you don't sell, you haven't lost a cent of "use value."

People often ask me if they can time the market to buy at the "perfect" price. My answer is always the same: **Forget it.** Timing the market is a fool's errand because the future is a black box. Instead of trying to be a "Genius Timer," you should aim to be a "Patient Owner."

The data backs this up. According to Redfin, the average homeowner now stays in their house for about **13 years**—double what it was back in 2005.[20] People have stopped treating their homes like a fast-food trade and started treating them like fortresses.

According to the Case-Shiller Index, it took about a **"decade"** for home prices to fully recover after the Great Financial Crisis.[21] It wasn't a smooth ride, but it proves a fundamental truth-**The market eventually rebounds.** By the time you're ready to pack up and move, the chance that your home will be worth less than its purchase price is low. It's not a guarantee, but it is a massive historical advantage for the patient "Dumb Investor."

- **Default Risk.** This is when the "Oxygen" runs out. If you lose your job or hit a rough patch, the bank doesn't care about your "long-term tenure"—they want their check. If you fall behind, you aren't just losing an asset; you're losing your fortress.

  Most people think they can just sell the house to pay back the loan if things get bad. But here is the "Chainsaw" trap: if you hit a rough patch at the same time the market crashes—like in 2008—you could find yourself with **zero equity.** You can't sell your way out of trouble because you owe the bank more than the house is worth.

Does this mean you should never buy a house? Nope. It just means you shouldn't try to be a "Genius" with your mortgage. You manage this risk by staying within your means and keeping your "Oxygen tank" (emergency fund) full. Historically, the market is a winner, but it only rewards the people who can afford to stay in their seats when the music stops.

USING LEVERAGE: PRIMARY RESIDENCE VS. INVESTMENT PROPERTY

To see the chainsaw in action, look at what happens when you use a 4-to-1 lever to buy two identical $200,000 houses—one to live in, and one to rent out. You put $40,000 down on each and borrow the rest from the bank.

	PRIMARY RESIDENCE	INVESTMENT PROPERTY
Purchase Price	$200,000	$200,000
Your Money (Down Payment)	$40,000	$40,000
Bank's Money (Borrowed)	$160,000	$160,000
Leverage	4 times	4 times

The Win. If the market ticks up by just 15%, the value of both houses hits $230,000. Because you only put $40,000 of your own skin in the game, that $30,000 gain feels like a miracle—you've nearly doubled your money (a 75% return) while the market barely moved.

The Kickback. Now, here's the scary part: if the market drops by 15%, your houses are worth $170,000. You've lost $30,000 of your original $40,000. In one bad move, **75% of your equity has vanished.** You're just one small tremor away from being "underwater," owing the bank more than the house is worth.

The Pressure Cooker. If you can keep making your payments, the "Safety Margin" we talked about earlier (the 13-year stay vs. the 10-year recovery) usually saves you. But here is the difference: **It's a lot harder to be patient with a rental property than it is with your own home**. When your house loses value, you still need a roof. But when an investment property starts bleeding cash or the market panics, you're tempted to run. This is the chainsaw cutting deep.

Other Market Traps. I've seen this same chainsaw in the world of stocks, futures, and margin accounts. They all promise the same thing—speed. But in the **Dumb Investor** system, we know that speed is the enemy of safety. If you decide to play with leverage, do it with your eyes wide open.

COMMANDMENT #5: DIVERSIFICATION

This is your "Anti-Catastrophe" insurance. You don't bet everything on one horse because you know that even the "sure things" can trip and break a leg. By spreading your bets across different industries, you ensure that a bad day for Tech or a meltdown in Banking doesn't take your whole portfolio to the grave. During the Dot-com crash or the 2008 collapse, the people who survived weren't the "Genius" stock-pickers; they were the "Dumb" investors who were spread out enough to keep breathing while everyone else was suffocating.

COMMANDMENT #6: EMOTIONAL DISCIPLINE

This is the hardest Commandment because it requires you to maintain your calm when your brain is screaming at you to run. The "Genius" investors think they can outsmart the market's mood swings, but the Dumb Investor knows that their own pulse is the biggest threat to their wealth.

If you can't watch your **"diversified"** portfolio turn bright red without hitting the "Panic" button, no strategy in the world can save you. You don't need a high IQ to build lasting wealth; you need the conviction to stay in your seat. Emotional discipline isn't about blindly holding a failing company to zero—it's about trusting that conviction and sticking to the broad-market plan you made when things were calm.

COMMANDMENT #7: ASSET ALLOCATION

If diversification is about not putting all your eggs in one basket, Asset Allocation is about deciding **how many eggs go into each.** Think of it as the master dial on your money machine. By splitting your money between stocks, bonds, and cash, you aren't just "managing risk"—you're making sure that when the stock market takes a dive, you still have enough "Oxygen" in your other pockets to keep breathing.

The Lesson. Your allocation is your personal **"Sleep at Night"** filter. A "Genius" investor might go 100% into the latest tech trend to chase a 50% return, but a **Dumb Investor** knows that a mix of assets is the only thing that keeps them in their seat when the market starts shaking. You don't allocate to be "perfect"; you allocate so you never have to break Commandment #1.

COMMANDMENT #8: TAX EFFICIENCY

Taxes are the ultimate "leak" in your investment tank. Every dollar you give to the government is a dollar that isn't compounding for you. The "Genius" investors spend thousands on lawyers to find complex loopholes, but a **Dumb Investor** simply uses the tax-free buckets the government literally hands to us.

The Advantage. In the US, tools like the 401(k), IRA, and 529 plan stop the government from siphoning off your gains before they have a chance to grow. You don't need a complex strategy to beat the tax man; you just need to use the buckets you were already handed.

SUMMARY

By now, you've started to get familiar with the core logic of this system. You have the **4Qs** (your Playbook) and the **Commandments** (your Rulebook) firmly in place. If you're like most people, you're likely checking your watch and eagerly waiting for the actual "answers." You want to know exactly what to buy and how to put this into practice right now.

In the chapters ahead, we are going to look at different kinds of moves and analyze the data to see which ones have historically stood the test of time. We'll also look at what the greatest investors in history have to say about them. Once we have the full picture of the market in front of us, we will put all these pieces together to build your own **"Money Machine."**

Tighten your seat belt—it's time to start the engine.

A Word from the Lawyers. I'm an author, not your personal advisor. Everything we just discussed—the 4Qs, the chainsaws, and the oxygen tanks—is for your education. This isn't a direct command for your brokerage account. Investing is a contact sport, and the risk of losing your principal is real. Before you swing the lever on your own money, make sure you've read the full "Universal Disclaimer" at the front of this book.

CHAPTER 2
THE ASSET CLASSES

Walk into any financial advisor's office, and they'll bury you in a mountain of options. It's meant to feel overwhelming. Honestly, I've sat through meetings where the jargon alone could make your head spin. They want you to believe the investment world is a complex labyrinth of stocks, bonds, mutual funds, commodities, and "alternative" derivatives that only a "Genius" can navigate.

But here is the secret: Most of that complexity is just clever marketing. Strip away the jargon, and you'll find that almost every investment on the planet is just a different version of a few basic building blocks. You don't need to master a thousand different "classes" to survive; you just need to understand the few that actually matter for your "stronghold."

EQUITIES

At its simplest, "Equity" just means you own a piece of the pie. If you put 20% down on a house, you own 20% of the bricks. In the stock market, it's the same thing—except the "house" is a massive corporation.

When you buy a share of a giant like Walmart or Microsoft, you aren't just betting on a ticker symbol. You are becoming a part-owner of their warehouses, their software, and their profits. You might only own a tiny fraction of the business, but as a **Dumb Investor**, you aren't trying to steer the ship; you're just hitching your wagon to a horse that already knows how to run.

HOW YOU GET PAID

When you buy a slice of Apple, you aren't just a fan of the iPhone; you're a beneficiary of every sale. If the company performs well, you generally get paid in two ways:

- **Appreciation.** This is the "Buy Low, Sell High" strategy. If Apple keeps churning out gadgets people can't live without, more investors will want a piece of the action, pushing the stock price up. If you bought in at $180 and the price hits $225, your slice of the pie is now worth 25% more. Of course, if it took ten years for that stock to move from $180 to $225, you didn't win—you barely kept pace with a savings account.
- **Dividends.** Think of this as a "Thank You" check from the company. After a giant like Apple pays its bills and reinvests in the next iPhone, it often has a pile of cash left over. Instead of sitting on it, they send a slice of those profits directly to you.

  The Math. Investors track this through the **Dividend Yield**. If a company sends you $2 for every $100 share you own, you're looking at a 2% yield. Just don't get too comfortable—Dividends are a gift, not a guarantee.

  The Yield Trap. As of late 2025, Apple's yield sat around 0.38%, while IBM's was over 2%. But don't let a higher number fool you into thinking IBM is the "better" horse.

A low yield, like Apple's, often means the company is using its cash to fuel a growth engine or buy back its own shares. A high yield can be a red flag; it might mean the company has run out of ideas on how to grow, or worse, that the stock price is crashing.

Remember the math: Since the stock price is the denominator, a crashing stock makes the yield look "better" on paper even as your investment is bleeding out. As a **Dumb Investor**, don't get blinded by the dividend check. Look for the **"Moat"**—the competitive wall that keeps the competitors away—and the demand for what they sell. A dividend is a nice bonus, but it won't save you if the "iPhones" stop selling.

SHARE BUYBACK: INCREASING YOUR PIECE OF THE PIE

A **buyback** is when the company uses its extra cash to buy its own shares and then effectively sets them on fire. I like to think of it as the company quietly giving you a bigger slice of the pie. By reducing the number of shares in the world, your piece gets more valuable without you spending an extra dime.

FIXED INCOME

If Equities means you own the pie, Fixed Income means you're the bank. I like to think of it as lending your money out and collecting rent. You aren't buying bricks or hiring CEOs; you're simply letting governments, big corporations, or banks borrow your cash. In return, they promise to pay you a fee—called interest—and eventually return your original money.

The Deal. These are called "Fixed" because the terms are set in stone from day one. You know exactly what the "Coupon" (the interest check) is and exactly when you'll get it.

The Risk. Don't be fooled by the name. While these are usually less of a rollercoaster than stocks, you're still betting that the borrower won't go bust. I've seen people get comfortable with bonds, only to get a rude surprise when the issuer runs out of cash. Then your "Fixed" income isn't fixed at all—it's gone.

BONDS

A bond is just a formal, tradable IOU. Think of it as lending someone money with a legal promise that they'll pay you back with interest. When a massive corporation or a government needs cash to build a bridge or a data center, they sell these IOUs to people like us.

Depending on who is asking for the money, the IOU gets a different name:

- **Corporate bond:** You're lending to a business.
- **Municipal bond:** You're lending to a local city or state.
- **Government bond:** You're lending to the country. In the U.S., these are **Treasuries**; in the UK or India, they are **Gilts**.

The Scale. Don't let the simplicity blind you. The world runs on these IOUs. As of year-end 2024, the total size of the global bond market was estimated at **$145.1 trillion**, with the U.S. market alone accounting for **$58.2 trillion**, according to the Securities Industry and Financial Markets Association (SIFMA).

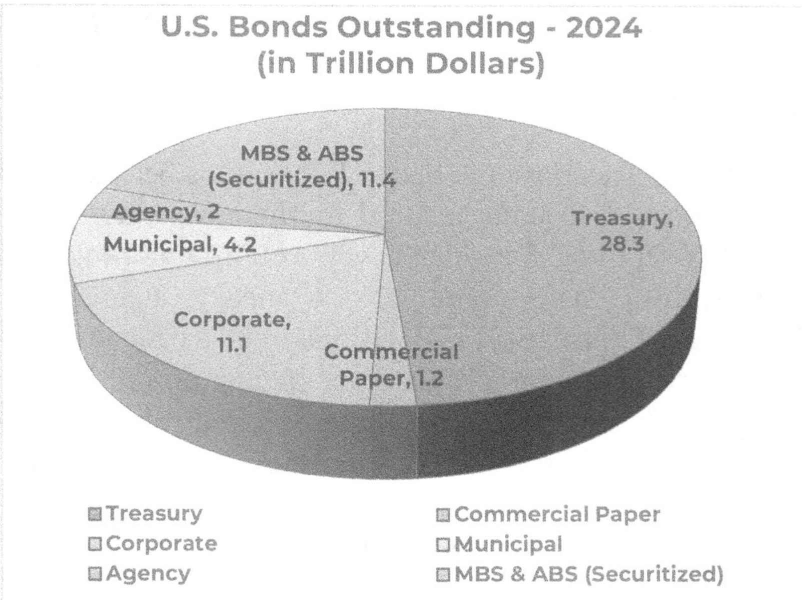

Source: SIFMA Research, 2025 Capital Markets Fact Book[22]

Don't let the "Fixed" label fool you; bonds get moody, too. We'll do a deep dive later in "***Bonds: The Fine Print***" to see why.

TIME DEPOSITS (CDS)

Think of this as putting your money in a vault and handing the bank the key for a set amount of time. Whether you call it a Certificate of Deposit (U.S.) or a Fixed Deposit

(India), the deal is the same: the bank gets to use your **"Fuel"** for a year (or three, or five), and in exchange, they pay you a higher rate than a standard savings account.

The Catch. The bank pays you more because you've promised not to touch the cash. If you change your mind and try to crack the vault early, they'll hit you with a **"Premature Withdrawal Penalty."** This isn't just a slap on the wrist; it can eat your interest and even bite into your original principal.

The Risk. These are the bedrock essentials because they are rock-solid—usually insured by the government (like the FDIC in the U.S., which covers you up to $250,000). But even a "safe" vault has a sneaky enemy—**the Inflation Termites**. I like to think of it as little invisible bugs slowly chewing away at your buying power. If your CD pays 5% but the termites are eating at 6%, you are technically getting "safer" and "poorer" at the same time. Your pile of cash looks the same, but the termites have hollowed out what that cash can actually buy.

The Math. Let's look at what actually happens when you lock $1,000 away at a 6% rate. On paper, it's simple math. But the frequency of the "payday" changes the size of your pile at the end.

- **The Simple Version (Annual Payday).** If the bank only checks the books once a year, they hand you $60 at the finish line. You walk away with $1,060.
- **The "Snowball" Version (Monthly Payday).** But banks are often more generous. They frequently compound interest monthly or even daily. This means

they pay you interest on your interest. It's a tiny difference at first, but it adds up.

To do the math, the bank simply takes your 6% annual rate and chops it into twelve monthly slices. Each month, you get one slice (0.5%) handed to you. Here is exactly how that $1,000 grows when your interest compounds every 30 days—essentially giving your "Snowball" a chance to roll and get bigger every single month.

The Snowball in Motion			
Month	**Starting Pile**	**Interest Earned**	**Ending Pile**
1	$1,000.00	$5.00	$1,005.00
2	$1,005.00	$5.03	$1,010.03
3	$1,010.03	$5.05	$1,015.08
...	...	...	...
6	$1,025.25	$5.13	$1,030.38
...	...	...	...
12	$1,056.40	$5.28	$1,061.68

The Win. By the end of the year, your monthly interest check has grown from **$5.00** to **$5.28**. Your money is quietly multiplying behind your back. You made an extra **$1.68** just because you let the bank pay you in slices instead of waiting for the whole pie at the end of the year.

APR VS. APY: THE MARKETING DANCE

Don't let the alphabet soup make your eyes glaze over. I promise, it's just a way for banks to dress up the same number.

APR (The Sticker Price). This is the raw annual interest rate. It's the "simple" number before the snowball starts rolling. In our CD example, the APR was **6%**.

APY (The Take-Home Pay). This is the "real" number. It accounts for all those monthly "slices" we talked about. Because your interest was busy having babies every month, you didn't just earn 6%; you earned **6.168%**. That's your APY.

The Hustle. Banks are smart. When they are **paying you** (like on a CD or savings account), they'll scream the **APY** from the rooftops because it's the bigger number. It makes their "vault" look more attractive.

But when you are paying them (like on a credit card), they usually highlight the **APR**. Why? Because it's the smaller number, and it makes the debt look less scary than it actually is.

The Label	The Number	The Reality
APR	6%	The "Sticker Price" (No Snowball)
APY	6.168%	The "Real Deal" (With the Snowball)

PICKING YOUR TERM

Choosing a CD term is a balancing act. You are trying to get the highest "rent" for your money without locking yourself out of the vault for too long.

The Rate Game. Usually, the longer you leave the keys with the bank, the more they pay you. But not always. Sometimes the bank's "Crystal Ball" tells them that interest rates are going to drop in the future, so they actually pay you *less* for a five-year lock-up than a one-year one.

The Exit Fee. Don't get blinded by a high rate on a 7-year CD. If life happens and you need that cash to keep your "Oxygen" levels up, the bank is going to make you pay to get back into your own vault.

REAL ESTATE: THE BIG KAHUNA

Real estate is the oldest, heaviest, and most popular way to store wealth on the planet. While the "Geniuses" obsess over ticker symbols and digital coins, more than half of the world's total wealth is sitting quietly in the dirt and the bricks.

The Physical Reality. Why is it so huge? Because you can touch it. You can live in it. I mean, try living in a Microsoft stock certificate. In the U.S. and the U.K., roughly two-thirds of people own the roof over their heads. In India, that number jumps to nearly 90%. Compare that to stocks, where most people wouldn't even know how to buy a share if you handed them the cash.

The "Dumb" Advantage. Real estate is the ultimate **Stronghold** because it's tangible. It doesn't vanish if the internet goes down or a CEO has a meltdown. To me, it's the one asset that keeps you grounded when everything else feels like digital smoke. It's "Real" in a way that "Paper" assets (stocks and bonds) never will be.

The Catch. Don't let the size of the market trick you—Real Estate has its own set of problems. It's a **Marriage, Not a Date.**

- **The Sluggish Exit.** You can sell a stock in a second. Selling a house takes months of paperwork and "Open

Houses." If a financial emergency hits and the housing market is having a "bad year," you can't just "withdraw" your cash. You are stuck in Concrete Boots.

- **The Hungry Asset.** Unlike a bond that pays you "rent," a house demands rent *from you* in the form of taxes, repairs, and insurance. It's one of the few assets that can actually cost you money just by sitting there.

If a financial emergency hits and the housing market is having a "bad year," you can't just "withdraw" your cash. You are stuck.

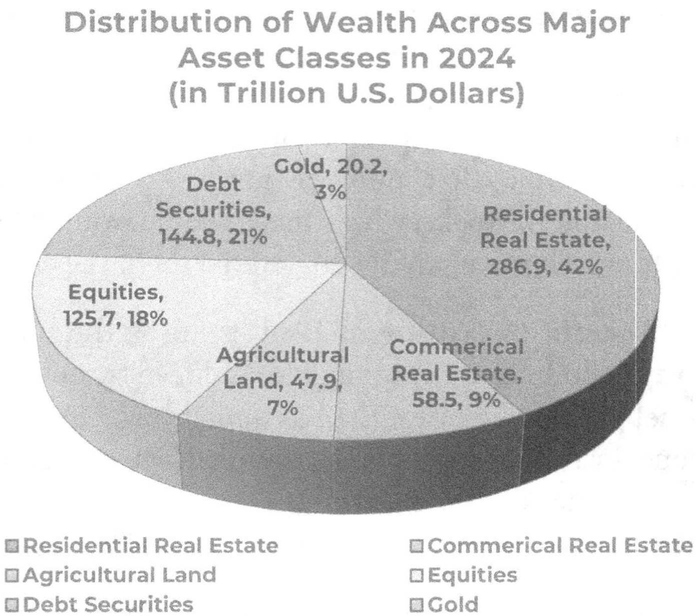

Source: Tostevin, Paul, & Rushton, Charlotte (October 2025), How much is global real estate worth?[23]

SUPER ASSET CLASS

Despite the "Concrete Boots," real estate remains the king of all asset classes for one simple reason: **It's the only investment you can't live without.**

Everybody Needs a Roof. You can survive your whole life without owning a single share of Apple or a government bond. But you can't survive without a roof over your head. This makes housing a **Basic Necessity**, not a luxury. This deep-rooted, universal demand is why I consider real estate the ultimate **Stronghold** for your cash. It's "resilient" because it's a biological requirement.

The Common-Sense Math. Evaluating a stock is like trying to read a CEO's mind—it's a "Genius" game of guesswork. But real estate? You already live in it. You know that a three-bedroom house in a quiet neighborhood is worth more than a one-bedroom apartment next to a noisy highway. Because the economics are **Physical**, you invest with a confidence you'll never find on Wall Street.

The "No More Dirt" Rule. The math is simple: the population is exploding, but the amount of land is fixed. God isn't making any more of it. When more people with more money chase a limited amount of dirt, prices have only one way to go over the long haul. As an owner, you're simply sitting on the right side of an unavoidable supply-and-demand trap.

The Warning. That confidence is exactly why people go "All-In" on property—which is why you must remain terrified of the **Chainsaw of Leverage.**

COMMODITIES: THE RAW STUFF

Commodities are the basic building blocks of life. We're talking about "The 3 Cs": **Crops, Crudes, and Coins.** This is wheat and cattle, oil and coal, gold and silver. Long before banks or stock markets existed, humans stored their wealth in the things they could eat, burn, or trade.

The Oil Boom. In the last century, oil became the "Black Gold" that built entire nations. Countries like Saudi Arabia and Qatar went from desert sands to global powerhouses overnight just by sitting on the right reservoirs. Even the U.S. and Canada saw their fortunes rise by pulling this energy out of the ground—I always find that part fascinating.

The Survival Warning. Here is the problem: Commodities are **"Unproductive Assets."** A house collects rent. A company grows profits and pays dividends. But a bar of gold or a barrel of oil just sits there. It doesn't grow; it doesn't "work" for you. It's only worth what the next guy is willing to pay for it. If the world decides it doesn't need as much oil because everyone is driving electric cars, your "Black Gold" becomes a liability fast.

The Price Rollercoaster. Because commodities are tied to forces like weather (crops), geopolitics (oil), and uncertainty (gold), their prices can be highly volatile. They don't move in smooth trends—they often jump in sharp, unpredictable spikes.

The Reality Check. Approaching commodities is like playing with fire. They're essential for the world, but dangerous if you're a **Dumb Investor** looking for safety. Since they don't produce an "income," you are essentially gambling that someone will be more desperate for that "Raw Stuff" tomorrow than you are today.

ONE COMMODITY TO RULE THEM ALL

If the world of commodities has a King, it's Gold. While oil moves us and wheat feeds us, Gold just... stays. It's the only asset that hasn't changed its "job description" in five thousand years. It doesn't rust, it doesn't rot, and it doesn't care who is President.

The Panic Button. Gold is the world's favorite "Safe Haven" because it's the ultimate hedge against human stupidity. When wars break out, when inflation eats the dollar, or when the "Geniuses" break the economy, people stop trusting paper and start trusting the shiny yellow metal. Even the biggest governments on earth—who print their own money—keep massive piles of gold in the basement "just in case."

The Golden Flaw. Before you go burying gold bars in your backyard, remember the "Unproductive" rule: **Gold doesn't work.** It just sits there looking pretty. It won't pay you a dividend, it won't pay you rent, and it won't grow. Its only value is the **"Greater Fool"** theory—you're betting that later on, someone will be more scared than you are and will pay more to take it off your hands.

How to Hold It. You have two choices here:

- **The Physical Way.** You can buy actual coins or bars. This feels great—until you realize you have to hide it, insure it, and worry about someone breaking in to take it.

- **The "Paper" Way (ETFs).** You can buy a "slice" of a giant pile of gold kept in a high-security vault through an **ETF** (Exchange Traded Fund). It's like owning gold without the headache of a home safe. It's faster, safer, and you can sell it with a click.

The Reality Check. Don't treat gold like a "get rich" scheme. Treat it like a **Fire Extinguisher.** You hope you never have to use it, but you're glad it's on the wall when the kitchen starts smoking.

COMMODITY FUTURES

Here's the thing—in the regular world, if you want oil, you pay the **"Spot Price"** (the price right now) and you get the oil. But in the world of the **"Geniuses,"** nobody actually wants the oil. They want to bet on what the oil will be worth six months from now. That is a **Future.**

The Price Lock. A futures contract is just a fancy way of saying "I promise to buy this stuff at this price on this date." It's like booking a hotel room a year in advance—you lock in the price today, hoping that by the time you show up, the room is worth twice what you paid.

The 10-Barrel Nightmare. Look at the fine print of a typical bet:

The Label	The Details
What	Crude Oil WTI
The Quote Date	January 1, 2024
The Locked Price	$60 per barrel

The Label	The Details
The Settlement	November 20, 2030
The Catch	10 Barrels
The Address	Cushing, OK

The "Get Out" Rule. Here is the scary part: if you hold that contract until the "Settlement Date" in 2030, you are legally required to show up in Oklahoma and take delivery of 10 barrels of crude oil. Unless you have a fleet of trucks and a massive storage tank in your backyard—who would want that?

To avoid the oil-on-your-lawn scenario, you have to **"Close your position"** before the deadline. You sell your "promise" to someone else. If the price of oil jumped to **$75** by the time you're ready to quit, you sell your $60 promise for a **$150 profit** ($15 x 10 barrels). You walk away with the cash; they deal with the barrels. Not bad, right?

THE SUPER-CHAINSAW

To understand futures, you first have to understand **Derivatives**. This is just a fancy financial term for a contract that "derives" its value from something else—like oil, gold, or wheat. You aren't buying the actual barrel of oil; you are buying a piece of paper linked to it.

Futures are the ultimate "Genius" trap because they are incredibly **Leveraged**. You don't have to pay the full **$600** for those 10 barrels upfront; you might only put down a **$50** deposit. Because you're so leveraged, even a tiny **1%** move in the price of oil acts like a sledgehammer to your account. It might double your money—or it might wipe out your entire **"Oxygen"** tank in a single afternoon.

Warren Buffett famously called these types of instruments **"financial weapons of mass destruction,"[24]** and he wasn't exaggerating. They are tools designed for professional gamblers and giant corporations. For the **Dumb Investor**, they are a trap. If you can't afford to watch your entire life savings vanish because of a pipeline leak or a war halfway across the globe, it's best to stay in the stands. These instruments aren't for protecting your wealth; they are for lighting it on fire.

WHO ACTUALLY NEEDS THIS STUFF?

While the **"Geniuses"** use futures to gamble, the people actually doing the work use them for one thing: **Sleep.** For the real world, the futures market is just a giant insurance policy against a chaotic future.

The Driller's Shield. Imagine you're pulling oil out of the ground today to sell in six months. If the price crashes tomorrow, you're ruined. By selling a "Future," you lock in today's price, guaranteeing your paycheck no matter what the market does.

The Airline's Budget. Airlines need millions of gallons of fuel. If oil spikes to $200, they can't raise ticket prices fast enough to stay in business. By buying a "Future," they lock in their costs years in advance. Their planes stay in the air because their price is already set in stone.

The Global Scoreboard. Because everyone is locking in these bets, the market creates a giant, real-time scoreboard. Financial types call this "**Price Discovery**," but really, it's just the world's most intense guessing game—like trying to predict tomorrow's weather with today's thermometer.

GOLD ON PAPER: THE ETF SHORTCUT

Back in 2004, the financial industry launched the first Gold ETF (called **GLD**).[25] It changed the game because it allowed regular people to own gold without the backache of actually carrying it or the stress of hiding it under a mattress.

The Golden Receipt. When you buy a share of GLD, you aren't buying a digital illusion. You are buying a "receipt" for real, physical gold bars sitting in a high-security vault at HSBC Bank. You own the gold; they just hold the keys.

The Math Check. The logic is simple: the total value of all the shares in the market should exactly match the value of the gold in the vault. As of early 2026, the numbers look like this:

The Asset	The Value (Feb 2026)
Gold in the Vault	34.9 million ounces
Price of Gold	$4950.50/oz
Total value of metal	$173 billion
Total value of shares	$173 billion

The "Vault Tax." You might notice that the ETF returns are always *slightly* lower than the return of raw gold.

Period	**GLD** (ETF)	**GOLD** (The Metal)
5-year total return	170.1%	178.5%
10-year total return	315.4%	330.4%
15-year total return	249.2%	267.2%

Source: World Gold Trust Services, LLC. "SPDR Gold Shares (GLD) Historical Data" (2026)[26]

Why the gap? Because the bank doesn't guard your gold for free. They charge a small management fee(**0.40% annual fee**)—think of it as **"Vault Rent."** You pay a tiny slice of your profit to avoid the headache of storage, insurance, and the risk of someone kicking in your front door. For the **Dumb Investor**, that's a trade-worth making every single time.

CASH: THE OXYGEN TANK

Every asset class we've talked about—Stocks, Bonds, Houses, and Gold—comes with a "Price Tag of Chaos." Their value dances around every single day. Fine for your retirement fund. A disaster for your grocery money. You can't tell your landlord, *"I'll pay the rent when the S&P 500 stops crashing."* Believe me, they won't wait.

The Survival Stash. For your everyday bills and your "Rainy Day" fund, you need assets that are boring, predictable, and fast. You need **"The Oxygen Tank."** This is money that doesn't "grow"—it just stays there, waiting for you to breathe it in when you need it.

The Oxygen Menu. This includes two things:

- **Cold Cash.** This is the physical currency in your wallet and the "Digital Cash" sitting in your checking and savings accounts. It's the fastest money on earth.
- **Cash Equivalents.** These are "Short-Term" IOUs—typically three months or less. Think of them as **"Almost-Cash."** Examples include **T-Bills**

(Government IOUs), short-term corporate paper, and money market funds. They are incredibly safe and easy to turn into "Real Cash" in a hurry.

WHERE TO PARK YOUR OXYGEN

Not all bank accounts are created equal. Some are for "Right Now," some are for "Just in Case," and it helps to know which is which.

The Wallet (Checking). Your financial front door. This is where your salary lands and your bills leave. It's built for speed, not growth.

- **The Catch:** Banks usually pay you **0% interest** here and might even charge you "Maintenance Fees" if you let the balance drop too low. It's essential, yes—but I wouldn't trust it to store any real wealth.

The Side-Pocket (Savings). This is where you separate your "Spending Money" from your "Survival Money."

- **The Traditional Trap:** Big-name banks are notorious for paying "Insult Interest"—around **0.01%**. That's not an investment; it's a rounding error.
- **The Digital Edge:** In early 2026, High-Yield Savings Accounts (HYSAs) are paying **3.0% to 4.0%**. It's the same safety, but the bank actually pays you for the privilege of holding your cash. Pretty good, huh?

The Hybrid (Money Market). Think of this as a "Checking Account with Muscles." You get the higher interest of a savings account (around 4.2% in early 2026) while keeping the "Check-Writing" powers of checking.

Perfect for managing a chunk of cash you might need to move fast.

THE UNCLE SAM GUARANTEE (FDIC)
If you put your money in a bank and that bank goes bust, who pays you back? That's where the **FDIC** comes in. It's an independent agency of the government that acts as the world's most powerful insurance policy for your cash.

What's Covered? It protects the "Oxygen": Checking accounts, Savings, CDs, and Money Market accounts.

What's NOT Covered? It won't cover your Stocks, Bonds, Mutual Funds, or Crypto. If those go to zero, you're on your own.

The $250,000 Rule. The government guarantees your cash up to **$250,000**, but they are very specific about how they count it. Think of it as $250k per bank, per "Bucket." [27]

The Bank	The Bucket	The Cash	The Guarantee
Chase Bank	Just You (Single)	$300,000	$250,000
Chase Bank	You & Spouse (Joint)	$550,000	$500,000 ($250k each)
American Express	Just You (Single)	$275,000	$250,000

The Bottom Line.

- **Spread it out:** If you have more than $250,000 in your own name, move the extra to a different bank.
- **Joint is better:** Putting your spouse's name on an account doubles your protection to $500,000.
- **Different Banks, Different Buckets:** Your limit at Chase has nothing to do with your limit at Amex.

The Hard Truth. The FDIC has been around since 1933, and in nearly a century, **no one has ever lost a single penny** of insured deposits.[28] It doesn't stop banks from being stupid and failing, but it makes sure their stupidity isn't your problem. If you want to sleep at night, just make sure your bank is on the list by using the **FDIC BankFind** tool.[29]

THE LAY OF THE LAND

We've just finished a tour of the world's giant money-storage lockers. By now, I hope you can look at a "Genius" in a suit and immediately tell what he's trying to sell.

- **Equities:** You're buying a slice of a "Money Machine."
- **Fixed Income:** You're the "Bank," collecting a "Thank You" check for lending your cash.
- **Real Estate:** You're betting on "The Only Thing They Aren't Making More Of."
- **Commodities:** You're playing with the "Raw Stuff"—great for survival, dangerous for gambling.
- **Cash:** Your "Oxygen Tank"—boring, but the only thing that matters when the room starts to smoke.

What's Next? In the next chapter, we're going to stop talking about "how" and start looking at the **Scoreboard.** We're going to dig into the history books to see which of these assets actually delivered the goods over the last century and which ones were just a lot of noise. It's time to see who actually won the race.

The Crypto Riddle—Digital Gold or Digital Dust?

You can't talk about money in 2026 without mentioning "magic internet coins." Since 2009, Bitcoin has become a trillion-dollar phenomenon, but for the **Dumb Investor**, it remains the ultimate "Genius" trap.

Is it actually money? Almost nobody uses Bitcoin to buy milk or pay a mortgage. It's a **Speculative Asset**—a "digital gold" that people buy only because they hope a bigger "Genius" will pay more for it next month. Its only superpower is **Digital Scarcity**: the government can print infinite dollars, but there will only ever be 21 million Bitcoins.

The Three Missing Anchors. This is why Warren Buffett famously said he wouldn't buy all the Bitcoin in the world for **$25**. It doesn't "do" anything. It lacks the three anchors that prove an asset is real:

- **No Cash Flow:** It's not a business. It doesn't sell products or pay dividends.
- **No Interest:** It isn't a bond; it doesn't pay you to hold it.

- **No Physical Use:** You can't burn it for heat, eat it for dinner, or wear it as a ring.

The "Secret Tunnel." Why the trillion-dollar price tag? Because it's a technological "Secret Tunnel"—a way to move wealth without a bank's permission. While great for freedom-seekers, it's also the preferred highway for **Digital Robbery** (ransomware) and **Hiding the Loot** (tax evasion).

The Hard Truth. Unlike the **US Dollar**, which is backed by "The House with the Army" (taxes, laws, and the military), Bitcoin is backed by **Code and Confidence**. I can't help but notice that it lives and dies by the crowd. If the crowd gets bored tomorrow, the floor doesn't just dip—it disappears.

The "Dumb" Take

We look for **Productive Assets**—things that grow corn or sell phones. Crypto is **Non-Productive**. It's not an investment in the economy; it's a bet that the digital crowd will keep growing. If you enter the tunnel, do it with your eyes wide open.

The Fine Print. I'm showing you how the financial machine works, not telling you exactly which levers to pull. This chapter is for **education**, not personalized advice.

Every person's situation is a different puzzle. What works for a billionaire might bankrupt a teacher. Before you bet your hard-earned cash, look at your own map: your goals, your age, and how much "market smoke" you can actually breathe. For the full legal details, check the **Universal Disclaimer** at the front of this book.

CHAPTER 3
THE GREAT ASSET RACE

In the last chapter, we looked at the "blueprints" for the world's different money lockers. You now know what they are and how they work. But now comes the million-dollar question: **Which one actually wins?**

It's time to stop talking about theories and start looking at the **Scoreboard**. We're going to look at how these assets actually behaved over the last century—through world wars, depressions, and tech booms—to see who delivered the goods and who was just a lot of noise.

THE CONTENDERS

To make this a fair fight, we're going to use the most trusted "measuring sticks" for each category:

- **Stocks (Equities):** We'll use the **S&P 500**. Think of this as the "All-Star Team" of the 500 biggest, most successful companies in America.
- **Houses (Real Estate):** We'll use the **Case-Shiller Index**.[30] This is the gold standard for tracking how much the average American home has gone up in value.
- **T-Bills:** The ultimate "Short-Term" IOU from the government (3 months). This is our baseline for "Safe Cash.

- **T-Bonds:** The "Long-Term" version of that government IOU (10 years).
- **Gold:** The world's oldest insurance policy.

The Source: Unless I tell you otherwise, all the numbers in this race come from **Aswath Damodaran** at NYU's Stern School of Business—the man the Wall Street calls "The Dean of Valuation."[31]

From 1928-2025

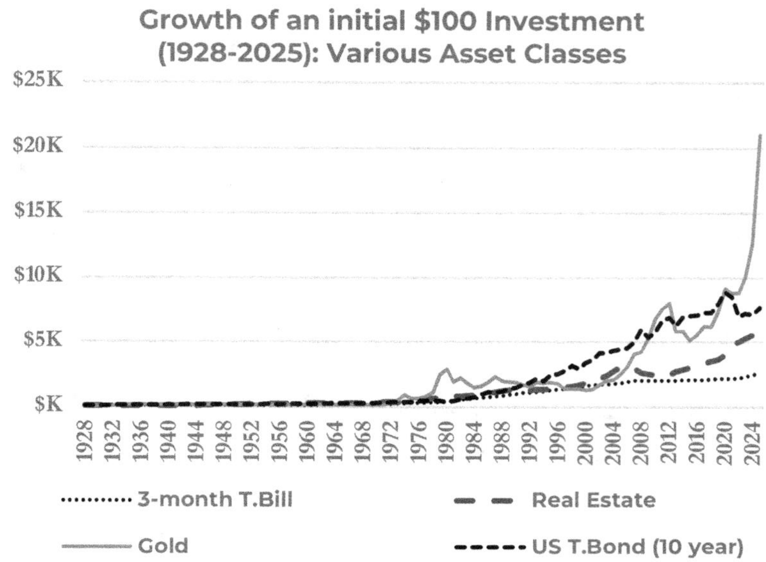

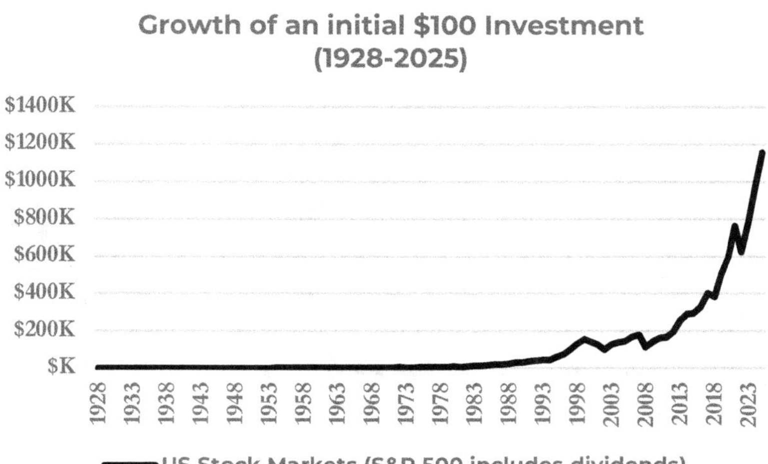

1928–2025 Results: The Winner: Your $100 in the **S&P 500** grew to **$ $1,157,009**. **The Runner-up:** Your $100 in **Gold** grew to **$21,025**.

From 1950-2025

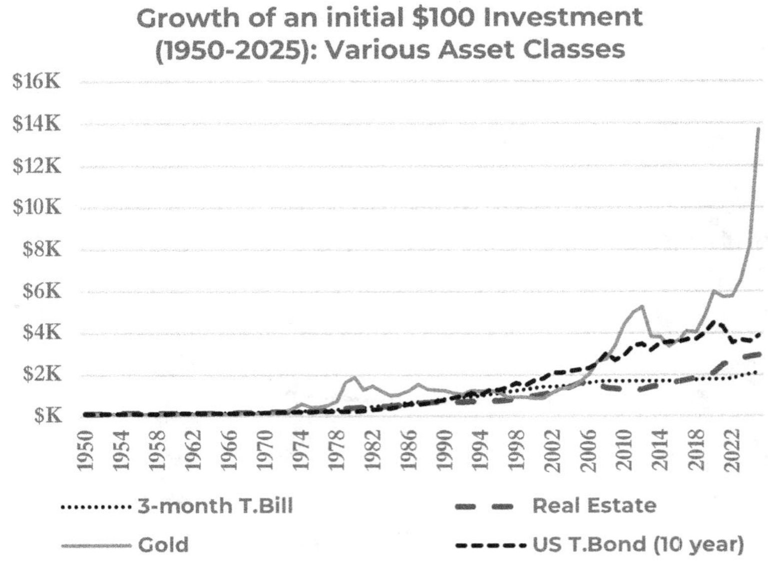

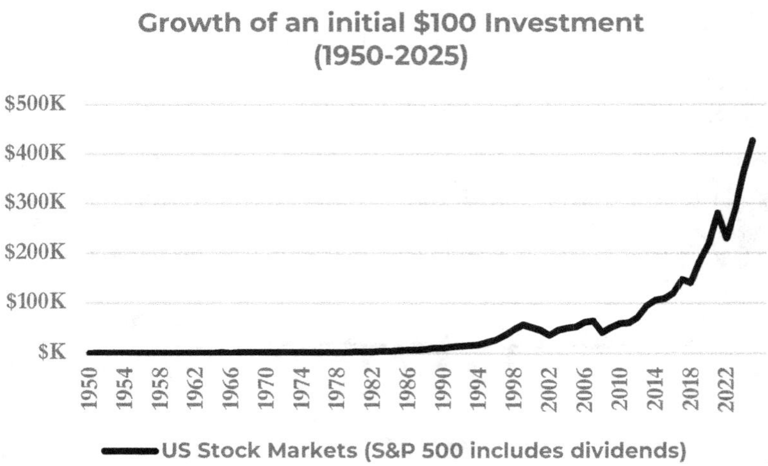

1950–2025 Results: The Winner: Your $100 in the **S&P 500** grew to **$425,603**. **The Runner-up:** Your $100 in **Gold** grew to **$13,694**.

From 1975-2025

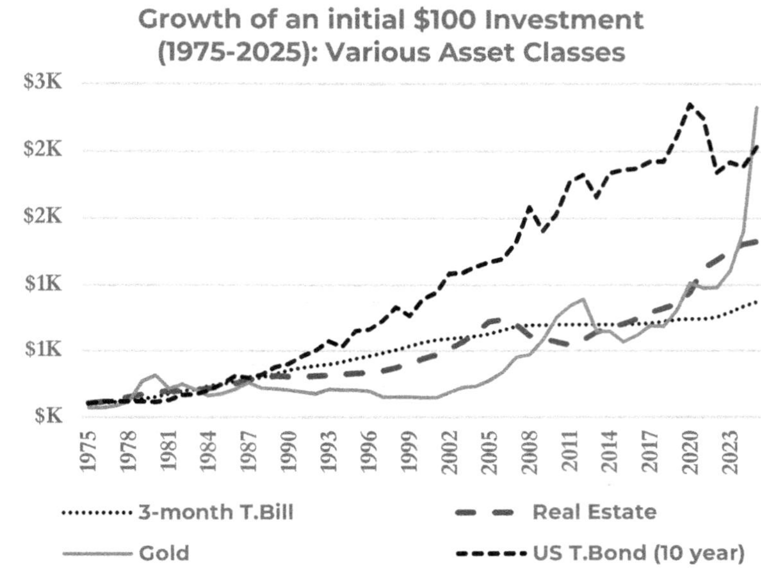

1975–2025 Results: The Winner: Your $100 in the **S&P 500** grew to **$38,267**. **The Runner-up:** Your $100 in **Gold** grew to **$2,327**.

From 2000-2025

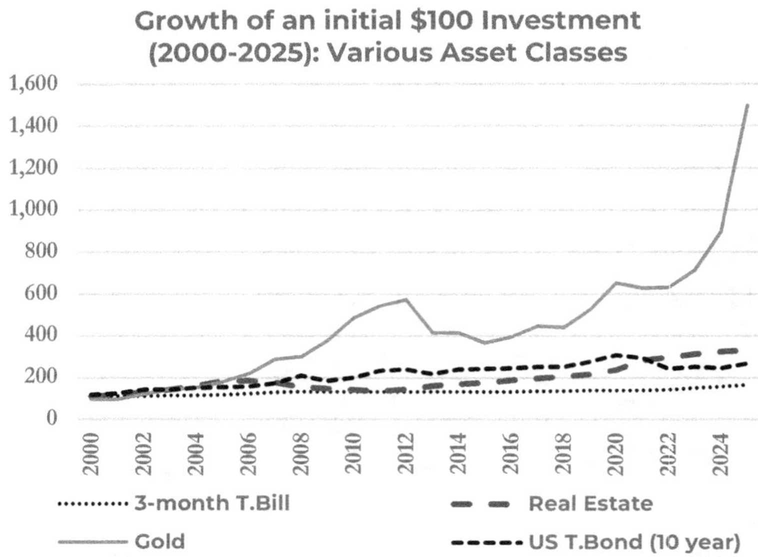

2000–2025 Results: The Winner: Your $100 in **Gold** grew to **$1,495**. **The Runner-up:** Your $100 in the **S&P 500** grew to **$739**.

THE VERDICT: THE CHAMPION VS. THE ROCK

If you look at the long-range scoreboard, Stocks (Equities) have spent a century crushing every other asset. But there have been several long stretches—like the 1930s, the 1970s, or the last 25 years—where Gold has actually taken the lead.

It makes you wonder, doesn't it? Has the "Money Machine" finally sputtered? Can a yellow rock really outpace a room full of CEOs? To answer that, we need to see why Gold caught a second wind.

WHY IS GOLD BEATING THE EQUITIES SO FAR IN THE 21ST CENTURY (2000-2025)?

The Lost Decade (2000-2009): The first ten years of this century were a disaster for stocks. It was the "Lost Decade." If you had dropped **$100** into the S&P 500 on New Year's Day in 2000, you would have ended the year 2009 with only **$90.86**. Between the "Dot-Com" bubble bursting and the "Great Financial Crisis" of 2008, the stock market was basically a boxing champion who spent ten years getting punched in the face. It happens—just ask anyone who lived through the **1930s**. [32]

The Panic Button: Gold is the world's favorite Panic Button. When the world feels like it's falling apart—wars, terror attacks, or banks collapsing—investors stop looking for "growth" and start looking for a "bunker." The 21st century has been a series of shocks. From 9/11 to global recessions, there has been a lot of "market smoke." And when the room gets smoky, people scramble for the one asset that has never gone to zero in 5,000 years.

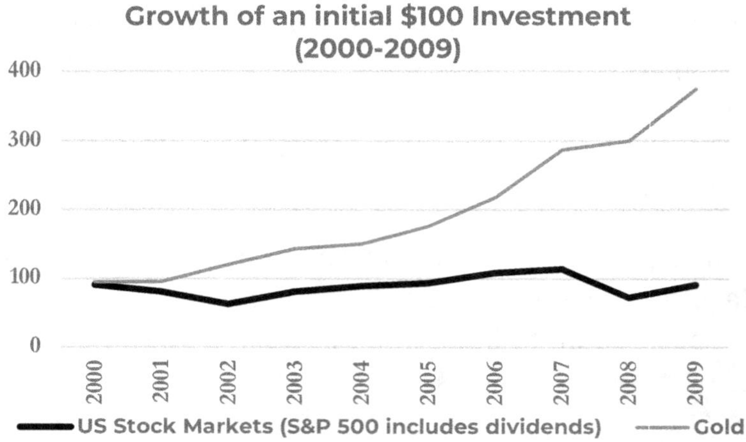

THE 90S PARTY: WHY THE START DATE MATTERS

If you want to make Gold look like a superstar, you start the clock in the year 2000. But if you back up just one decade to the 1990s, the story changes completely.

The 1990s Party. The 1990s was a decade where the "Money Machine" was firing on all cylinders. Stocks didn't just grow; they exploded. If you include that decade in the mix, the 21st-century "lead" that Gold currently enjoys starts to look like a rounding error.

Don't Judge the Marathon by One Mile. In the 2000s, stocks tripped over their own feet. It was a brutal decade. But since then, the S&P 500 has gotten back off the mat and started sprinting again. When you look at the big picture—including the 90s and the recovery after the 2008 crash—Stocks still hold the heavy-weight belt.

The Bottom Line. Gold is great for protecting your cash during a 10-year hangover (like the 2000s). But for building actual wealth over 20, 30, or 40 years, history suggests it's hard to beat a room full of people working hard to make a profit.

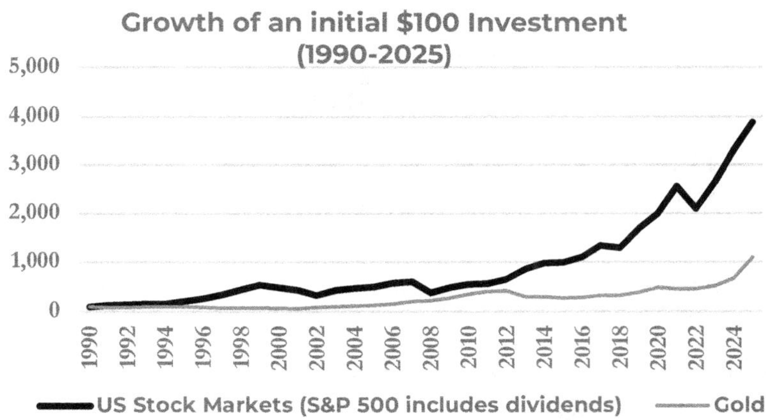

Excluding the 2000s

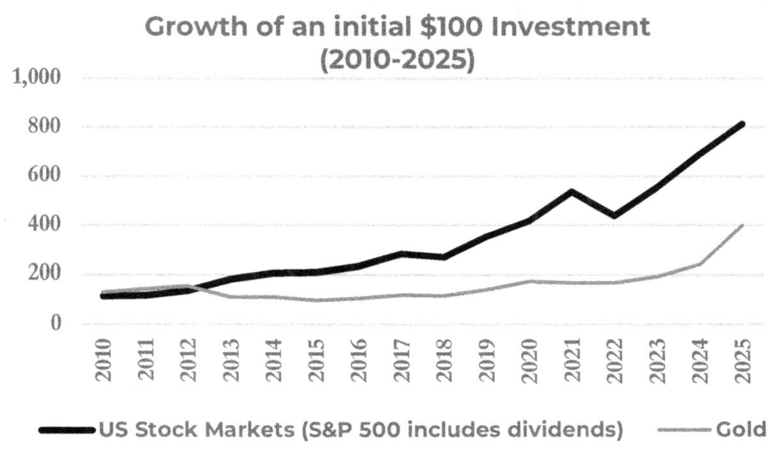

THE 1970S: SPINNING THE WHEELS

If you lived through the 1970s, you saw a decade where the "Money Machine" basically stalled out.

The Great Inflation Fire. The 1970s were a mess. Between oil shortages, the end of the Vietnam War, and the government changing the rules on how the dollar worked, inflation went through the roof. When the cost of everything—from milk to gasoline—is skyrocketing, it's hard for companies to make a real profit. Stocks spent the decade spinning their wheels, barely going anywhere.

The Golden Lifeboat. While stocks were struggling to stay afloat, Gold was having the time of its life. In a decade defined by uncertainty and "shrinking" dollars, people scrambled for something they could hold in their hands that wouldn't melt. Historically, when the "Fire" of inflation starts burning, Gold is the first thing people grab to save their wealth

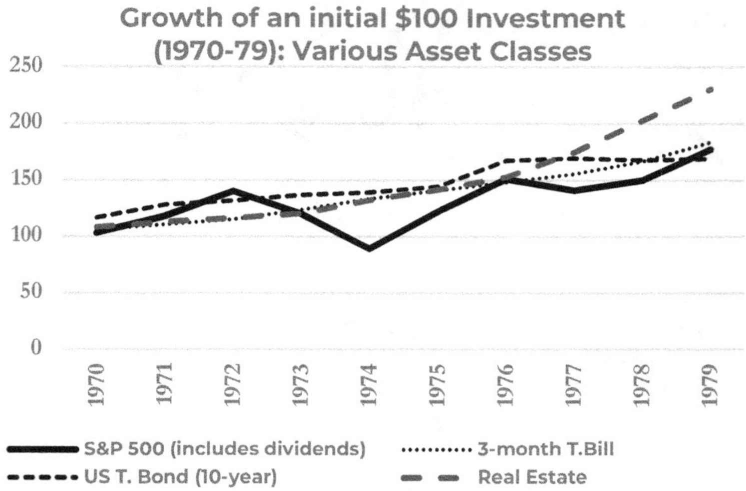

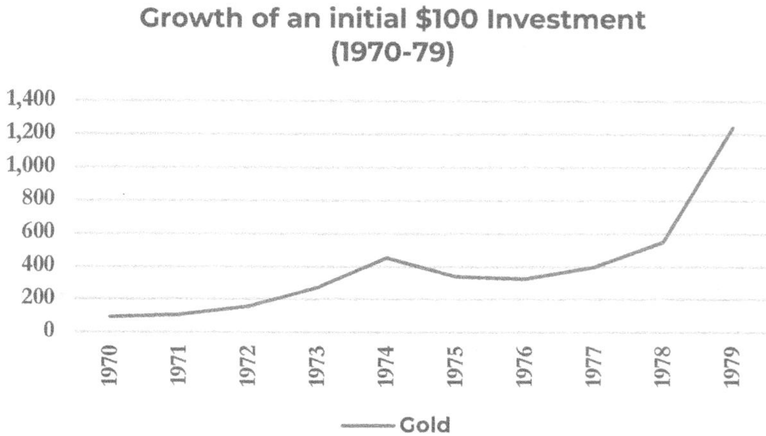

1930S: STUCK IN THE DITCH

If the 1970s was a car spinning its wheels, the 1930s was the car sliding off the road and landing face-first in a ditch.

The Great Depression. This was a brutal decade where the "Money Machine" essentially broke. After the 1929 crash, stocks spent ten years fighting just to climb back up to the pavement. It wasn't just a slow period; it was a total collapse of the system.

The Survival Asset. While the economy collapsed into bread lines, Gold was the only winner. As the chart shows, when the world feels like it's ending, people ditch the "Geniuses" and run straight for the yellow rock.

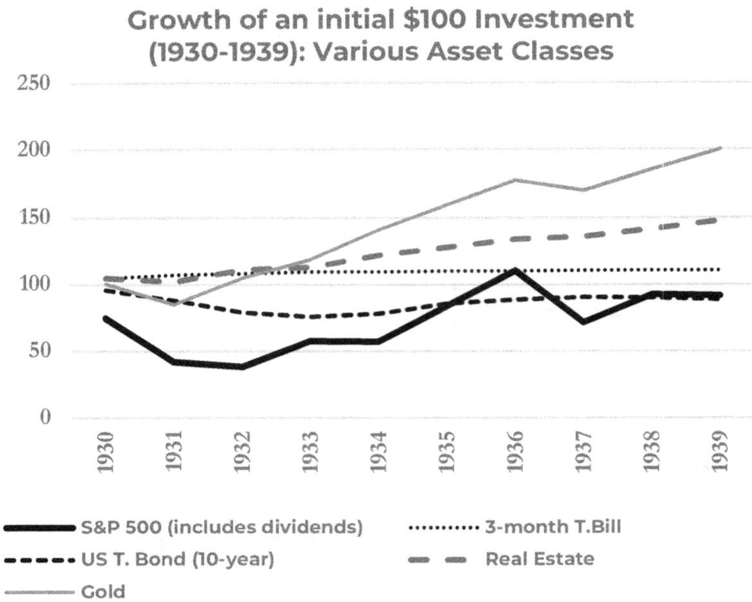

THE LONG VIEW: THE SURVIVAL RECORD

If there is one thing the history books tell us, it's that equities (stocks) aren't magic. They don't **outperform in every single period**. In fact, in the nine decades since the 1930s, stocks "lost" the race three times.

The Probability is in Your Favor. Even though they aren't perfect, the "Money Machine" still **emerged as the leader** in six out of those nine decades. Look at the last 25, 50, or nearly 100 years, and you'll see stocks consistently finish ahead of the pack.

The Marathon Rule. The most important thing to remember is that the longer the timeline, the more likely the "Machine" is to succeed. In a one-year sprint, anything can happen—gold might spike, or the economy might land in a ditch. But over 20, 30, or 40 years, the power of human productivity almost always leaves the "safety" assets in the dust.

The Catch. Just because the Machine has a great track record doesn't mean it's a sure thing. History is a guide, not a guarantee. There will be more **"Lost Decades"** and more **"Inflation Fires"** in the future. Your job isn't to predict when they happen, but to make sure you have enough gas—your emergency cash—in the tank to drive right through them.

A Quick Reality Check. This chapter is for **education**, not personalized advice. I'm showing you a map of where the money has gone in the past, not telling you exactly where to put your next paycheck.

History is a guide, not a guarantee. While the S&P 500®, Gold, and Bonds have a 100-year track record, market rules can change, and you can still lose money. Every situation is a different puzzle, so please check the **Universal Disclaimer** at the front of this book for the full legal details.

CHAPTER 4
THE TWO WAYS TO PLAY

By now, you've seen the 100-year track record. You know the "Money Machine" usually leads the pack. But knowing the machine works is one thing; deciding how you're going to drive it is another. When you strip away the jargon, there are really only two ways to operate the machine. I call them the **Sprinters** and the **Marathoners**.

TRADING: THE ART OF THE GUESS

When people talk about "Trading," they are really talking about being a **Sprinter**. Traders aren't looking to own a company for twenty years; they want to profit from the world's mood swings. They don't care where a business will be in a decade; they care where the price is going in the next ten minutes, days, or months.

Chasing the Shock. The stock market is basically a giant thermometer for human emotion. When something big happens, the mercury moves fast.

- **The Bad Days.** On November 22, 1963, when JFK was assassinated, the S&P 500® dove nearly **3%**.[33] The same thing happened after Pearl Harbor and 9/11. It's the "Panic Button" in action—when people are scared, they sell first and ask questions later.
- **The Good Days.** On the flip side, moments like the end of World War II or the Moon landing sent a surge

of "market adrenaline" through the system, pushing prices up as everyone felt invincible.

The Product Hype. Traders spend their lives trying to jump in front of these moves. They watch for moments that grab the world's attention—like when Apple unveiled the first iPhone in 2007 or Tesla showed off the Model S in 2012. They are trying to guess how the crowd will react before the crowd even knows what it's feeling.

The "Math Wizards" vs. The Crowd. Trading isn't just a hobby; it's an **Arms Race**. On one side, you have individuals looking at charts (Technical Analysis) to spot patterns in the chaos. On the other, you have billion-dollar hedge funds hiring "Math Wizards" to build high-speed "Robo-Traders" that buy and sell in fractions of a second. Whether they are "Scalping" (seconds) or "Swing Trading" (weeks), these people aren't looking at the soul of a company. They are looking at the math of the move.

THE "DUMB" TAKE. Trading is like trying to catch lightning in a bottle—sometimes you get the spark, but often you just get burned. You are trying to predict which way a leaf will blow in a hurricane. You can use all the math and charts you want, but at the end of the day, you are betting on the most unpredictable thing on earth: **Human Behavior**. It's high-speed, high-stress, and for most regular people, it's a great way to lose a lot of money very quickly.

FAMOUS (AND INFAMOUS) BETS

Trading is a high-octane pursuit where you can become a legend or a cautionary tale overnight. It's not about "steady growth"; it's about catching the big move when it happens.

The Man Who Broke the Bank. In 1992, George Soros made one of the most famous bets in history. He realized the British Pound was "inflated"—like a balloon ready to pop. He bet billions that it would crash. When it did, on a day now called **"Black Wednesday,"** he walked away with a billion-dollar profit.[34] It's the ultimate "Sprinter" payoff, but remember: if the balloon hadn't popped, he would have been the one left holding the bill for billions.

The London Whale. Not every big swing hits the mark. In 2012, a trader at JP Morgan—nicknamed the **"London Whale"**—made a bet so massive it actually started moving the entire market.[35] But the tide turned against him. What started as a "protection plan" ended up sinking the ship, costing the bank over **$6 billion**.

The takeaway? The bigger the potential prize, the sharper the cliff you're standing on.

THE SAFETY NET: RISK MANAGEMENT

Because the market is unpredictable, professional traders don't just "hope for the best." They use a toolkit to make sure a single bad guess doesn't wipe them out. Think of these as the **Brakes, Seatbelts, and Airbags** of the trading world:

The Stop-Loss (The Brakes). This is a pre-set command that says, "If this stock drops to $90, sell it immediately." It's designed to stop the bleeding before a small skid turns into a total wreck.

Profit-Taking (The Seatbelts). It's easy to get greedy when a stock is climbing, but gravity always wins eventually. Profit-taking is the discipline of "buckling in" your gains by selling some of your winners while you're ahead. That way, if the market suddenly hits a wall, you don't fly through the windshield.

Position Sizing (The Airbags). This is the ultimate "cushion." It's the rule of never putting so much money into one single "guess" that a failure ruins your life. If one trade goes to zero, your "airbags" deploy because that trade was only a tiny fraction of your total cash. It stings, but you walk away from the crash.

INVESTING: THE MARATHONER

If Trading is a high-speed sprint, **Investing** is the long-distance haul. Marathoners aren't trying to outsmart the daily news cycle or catch a "vibe." They buy a slice of human productivity and let it grow for decades while they get on with their lives. Sure, the "Money Machine" might hit a pothole this month, but it's still the best vehicle to carry you across the finish line twenty years from now.

Looking Under the Hood. To a Marathoner, a stock isn't just a flashing number on a screen–it's a living, breathing business. Before they buy, they use "Fundamental Analysis" to see if the engine is actually solid. Here's what they look at:

- **The Price Tag (P/E Ratio).** Shows how much the market charges for each dollar of profit. Think of it as the "Is this overpriced?" check.

- **The Spare Parts Value (P/B Ratio).** Compares the stock price to the company's physical stuff—buildings, equipment, inventory. Helps you see if you're paying for actual "parts" or just a fancy logo.
- **The Sticker Price (Enterprise Value).** The real cost of buying the whole business, including debt. Like checking the price of a house plus the mortgage you'd take on.
- **The Spendable Cash (Free Cash Flow).** The actual cash left in the register after bills are paid. It's what the company can use to pay dividends or grow.
- **The Efficiency Grade (ROE).** Shows how much profit the company squeezes out of shareholder money. A measure of whether the "Geniuses" running it are actually good at their jobs.
- **The Debt Load (Debt-to-Equity).** Tells you if the business stands on solid ground or a mountain of borrowed money.

The Growing Garden. Being a Marathoner is about discipline. You aren't reacting to every "breaking news" alert or political scandal. You treat your portfolio like a **growing garden**—recognizing that you can't scream at a seed to make it grow faster. Real results take time, consistency, and the patience to ignore the market's noise.

MR. MARKET'S MOOD SWINGS

The market isn't a cold, calculating machine. It's more like the partner Benjamin Graham described in his classic, *The Intelligent Investor*. He called him **Mr. Market**—a guy who is brilliant one day and totally unhinged the next.[36]

Every day, Mr. Market shows up at your door with a price. Sometimes he's in a state of **Euphoria**, telling you your business is a gold mine and offering you a fortune. Other times, he's gripped by **Fear**, convinced the world is ending, and offering to sell you his share for pennies.

The Voting Machine vs. The Weighing Machine. Graham had another famous rule for dealing with this erratic partner:

> **In the short run, the market is a voting machine, but in the long run, it is a weighing machine.**[37]

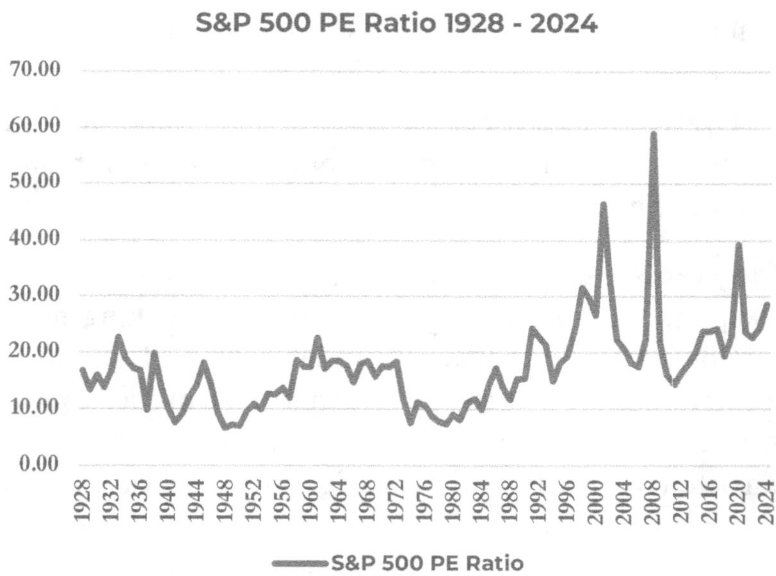

Source: Robert J. Shiller, Price Earning Data.[38]

MR. MARKET'S MELTDOWNS ARE YOUR OPPORTUNITIES

The chart above shows the P/E Ratio in action. Think of this as the market's Thermometer. As you can see, the "temperature" is never a straight line; it's a jagged mess of spikes and dips. Those spikes and dips happen for a million different reasons, but they all tell the same story: Mr. Market is almost never level-headed. The best part about having an unhinged partner like Mr. Market is that, every once in a while, he hands you a gift. Savvy investors don't get scared when the crowd starts panic-voting; they go shopping.

The Apple Bet. Take Warren Buffett. In early 2016, the "Voting Machine" was turned against Apple. People were worried that everyone who wanted an iPhone already had one and that the company had run out of ideas. Mr. Market was having a bad day, and the stock price reflected it.

While the "Geniuses" predicted doom, Buffett looked under the hood. He didn't see a tech company in trouble; he saw one of the strongest brands on the planet with a "sticky" ecosystem that people couldn't live without. Recognizing Mr. Market's irrational mood, he started buying. He didn't just dip a toe—he backed up the truck, turning it into one of investing's biggest wins. [39]

Buffett's Purchase of Apple (early 2016 to mid-2018)

Apple Stock Price 2013-2019

Source: macrotrends.net[40]

THE SURVIVAL GUIDE

Investing is a journey into the unknown. You can't control the market's mood, but you *can* control how you build your boat.

Don't Bet on One Horse. If you put all your cash into one company and it hits an iceberg, you're going down with the ship. By spreading your money across different businesses (**Diversification**), one bad apple won't spoil your whole harvest.

The Emergency Bunker. Life will eventually throw you a curveball—a job loss or a surprise bill. Without a cushion of cash, you might have to sell stocks at a loss just to survive.

The Goal is Survival. Risk management isn't about fear; it's about making sure you never have to quit the race.

TRADING, INVESTING, AND THE MESSY MIDDLE

It's easy to box these into two categories: hold for a day and you're a **Trader**; hold for a decade and you're an **Investor**. But in real life, the lines blur. There is a massive "grey area" in the middle where the two overlap.

Some people find the high-speed chase of trading too stressful, while others find long-term investing too slow. You might use a bit of both—checking charts for a good entry while planning to stay for the long haul. Ultimately, you'll settle on whatever style lets you sleep at night without checking your phone every few minutes.

The "Let it Go" Factor. No matter your style, the market will eventually punch you in the face. It's part of the game. I've seen people lose their minds over a 5% dip and others stay calm through a 50% crash. The secret isn't having a perfect strategy; it's having a "Dumb" level of discipline.

You have to learn to accept losses with humility and gains without ego. Even the legends have been humbled by the market. Navigating those storms calmly—practicing a philosophy of "letting it go"—is often the only difference between the person who finishes the race and the person who quits in a panic.

The stock market, much like life, is a series of ups and downs. If you can't handle the downs, you don't deserve the ups.

TRADING VS. INVESTING AT A GLANCE

To summarize, the following are the key differences between trading and investing.

The Metric	Trading (The Sprinter)	Investing (The Marathoner)
The Goal	Catching a "wave" to make a quick buck.	Buying a business to build wealth over time.
Timeline	Minutes, days, or maybe a few months.	Years or decades.
Homework	Watching price charts and the news cycle.	Checking the "engine" (profits and products).
Safety Gear	Brakes, Seatbelts, and Airbags.	Not putting all your eggs in one basket.
The Risk	High-octane; one wrong guess can be a wreck.	Market "potholes," but time heals most wounds.

WHY THE WINNER'S CIRCLE IS SO SMALL

If making money in the market were easy, everyone would be doing it from their couch in their pajamas. The reality? Most people struggle. Here's why the "Money Machine" trips up the average investor.

- **Your Biology is a Bottleneck.** It is incredibly difficult to behave rationally and maintain your calm during Mr. Market's mood swings. We are hardwired to seek safety in the herd. When the market turns bright red, your DNA will scream at you to follow the crowd and run for the exits. On the flip side, when the "Voting Machine" is in a state of euphoria, that same instinct will tempt you to abandon your plan and chase the hype.

- **The "True Worth" Guessing Game**. No business comes with a magic price tag. You can look at the "Sticker Price" (Enterprise Value) or the "Spendable Cash" (Free Cash Flow), but those numbers change. And how do you measure a company's "soul" or the quality of its people? You can't. Every investment is still an educated guess.
- **It's a Business, Not a Video Game**. Too many treat the stock market like a casino or a video game—press a button, make money. They see ticker symbols ($AAPL, $TSLA) instead of real buildings, real employees, and real products. If you don't treat a stock as **ownership in a real business**, you aren't investing—you're just gambling on letters and numbers.
- **The "Perfect Timing" Trap**. We've all felt it—that gut punch of regret after selling a stock too early or holding on while it sinks like a stone. Most people spend their lives trying to "time" the market, hunting for the perfect bottom or the exact peak. Here's the truth: nobody knows where the floor or the ceiling is. Even the professionals get it wrong. Trying to time the market is like trying to catch a falling knife; you might get lucky, but you're more likely to end up in the ER.
- **The Herd Mentality.** We're wired to follow the pack. At a barbecue, a "hot tip" feels safe. But in the market,

the crowd is often last to know and first to panic. Independent thinking is your only armor. As Warren Buffett says:

> **Everybody, when they buy a stock, should be able to take a yellow pad and write down exactly why they plan to invest in that particular company**[41]

By thinking independently and basing your decisions on careful analysis, you can avoid the pitfalls of blindly following the crowd.

- **The Cost of Fear.** Some are so scared of the "Money Machine" they never even flip the switch. Headlines and horror stories keep them on the sidelines. Cash may feel "safe," but over time, it's a slow-motion disaster. By letting fear keep you out, you miss the market's greatest force: **compounding**. Over decades, being out of the market is often riskier than being in it.

SUMMARY: PICKING YOUR PLAY

In this chapter, we've looked at the two ways to navigate the arena: **Trading** (The Sprinter) and **Investing** (The Marathoner). They aren't just different strategies; they are different worlds. One is about catching lightning in a bottle; the other is about planting a garden and having the patience to watch it grow.

By now, you should see that making money in the market isn't about finding a "secret button." It's a gritty, challenging pursuit that takes more than just a laptop and a dream. It takes a "backbone" to stay steady when the red numbers start flashing and the "stomach" to ignore the crowd when they're screaming.

The Danger of the High. It's easy to feel like a genius when the market is going up. Everyone looks like a pro when the wind is at their back. But the real test happens when the wind shifts. I'll leave you with a warning from the master himself, Benjamin Graham:

> **While enthusiasm may be necessary for great accomplishments elsewhere, on Wall Street it almost invariably leads to disaster.**[42]

A Quick Reminder. This chapter is about understanding how the "Machine" works, not a set of instructions for your own money. There are no "cheat codes" here, and history doesn't always repeat itself. Whether you're a Sprinter or a Marathoner, the market is a high-stakes environment where it's entirely possible to lose every cent you put in.

Your situation is unique. Think for yourself, know your own limits, and never bet more than you can afford to lose. For the full, "suits-and-ties" legal details, please refer to the universal disclaimer at the beginning of the book.

CHAPTER 5
WHY THE HASSLE? LET THE PROS DRIVE

After everything I've shown you so far, you're probably asking the obvious question: If the market is a "**moody partner**" and picking stocks is a full-time job, why not just hire a pro to do it for me?

Most people tackle this in two ways:

The Travel Agent (Financial Advisors). You hire someone to sit across the table from you, look at your life, and map out the trip. But here's the thing: most advisors aren't actually under the hood picking individual stocks. Instead, they're navigators—they help you choose the right Deluxe Bus to get on. You're often paying two sets of fees here: one for the agent to show you the map, and one for the chauffeur driving the bus.

The Deluxe Bus (Mutual Funds). This is the direct route. Instead of driving your own car through the market's potholes, you "pool" your money with thousands of other people and hop on a Deluxe Bus. This bus is managed by a **Chauffeur** (a professional fund manager). In the U.S. and India, we call these **Mutual Funds**; in the UK, they're **Unit Trusts**. The idea is simple: you provide the gas money, and they handle the steering.

I've learned that before you hand over your hard-earned cash to a professional, you need to understand exactly what kind of **"Deluxe Bus"** you're getting on and—more importantly—how much the **"Chauffeur"** is charging you to sit in the seat.

ENTER THE "VILLAGE POOL"

To understand how a Mutual Fund actually works, imagine a village full of people like us— "Dumb" Investors. We all have a little bit of money, but none of us have the time or the "stomach" to watch the market all day.

In this village lives **Mr. Smart**, a guy who eats, sleeps, and breathes the stock market. So we huddle up and throw our money into one big bucket: **The Village Pool Fund**. We hand the bucket to Mr. Smart and tell him to go to work.

I've looked at the rules for these "Pools," and they usually go something like this:

- **The Goal.** Mr. Smart's job is to grow the bucket over the long haul. No get-rich-quick schemes—just slow, steady growth.
- **The Strategy.** He isn't going to gamble on "penny stocks" or fly-by-night companies. Instead, he buys the "**Blue Chips**"—the big, sturdy companies that everyone knows and trusts.
- **The "Paycheck".** This is the part you need to watch. Mr. Smart charges a **2% annual fee** to hold the bucket. If the bucket is worth $100,000, he takes $2,000 for himself every year. And here's the kicker:

he takes this cut whether the fund goes up or down. Even if he loses half your money, he still gets paid.

- **The Scoreboard.** We compare Mr. Smart's performance to the **S&P 500**. This is his "Benchmark." If the rest of the market goes up 10% but Mr. Smart only delivers 5%, he's basically a slow driver in a fast lane.
- **The Open Door.** There's no "VIP list." Anyone in the village can toss in as little as $1. It's the ultimate "Money Machine" for the little guy.

WHY THE VILLAGE POOL WORKS

- **You Hire a Pro:** You get Mr. Smart's brain without having to.
- **Wholesale Pricing.** By pooling your cash, you get a "bulk discount" on trading costs. It's a lot cheaper to buy a thousand shares as a group than for everyone to buy one share individually.
- **Safety in Numbers.** Even if you only put in $100, your money is spread across 50 or 100 different companies. If one company in the bucket goes bust, the other 99 keep the bucket afloat.

THE STICKY BITS (WHAT MR. SMART CAN'T FIX)

- **The "When" Problem:** Mr. Smart manages the bucket, but *you* still have to decide when to jump in and when to climb out. If you hire an advisor to help you time it, be careful. **Let me caution you:** Some advisors get paid more to steer you toward certain buckets. If their "expert advice" sounds like a sales pitch, it probably is.

- **The Panic Factor:** I see it all the time—the market dips, the villagers lose their nerve, and they pull their money out of the pool at exactly the worst moment. Mr. Smart can't stop you from hitting the "eject" button if you lose your cool.
- **Following the Pack:** Just because everyone else in the village is jumping into the pool doesn't mean it's a good time to get wet. The "Herd" is usually loudest right before the market hits a pothole.

THE NEW HEADACHES

- **The "Invisible" Tax.** Mr. Smart's 2% fee might not sound like much, but it's a slow leak in your bucket. In the real world, these funds have all sorts of fancy labels for putting their hands in your pocket—management fees, admin costs, "sales loads." To me these fees are like termites; you don't see them working, but over a decade, they can eat through a huge chunk of your wealth. These costs take a bite out of your returns before you ever see a dime.
- **The Choice Paralysis.** It's wild when you think about it. As of early 2025, there were over 4,000 mutual funds in the U.S. alone.[43] To put that in perspective, there are almost as many "Chauffeurs" out there as there are actual companies to invest in on the big exchanges.

Clearly, picking a mutual fund can be as daunting as choosing a stock to invest in.

I'll show you how to simplify this later, but for now, just know that "more choice" often just means more ways to get lost.

A HALFWAY HOUSE

Mutual funds are a step in the right direction, but they aren't a magic wand. They're like a "halfway house"—you're off the street, but you aren't home yet. You can still make all the classic mistakes: you can overpay, you can panic at the wrong time, and you can still pick a driver who doesn't know where he's going. They offer a partial solution, but the "Dumb" Investor still needs a better map.

THE DIFFERENT FLAVORS OF FUNDS

One thing I had to wrap my head around early on is that things like Mutual Funds or ETFs aren't "investments" in the same way a stock is. They are just **containers**. They are the buckets or "buses" we use to carry our money into the market.

The way I see it, you can put almost anything into these containers. Here is how they are usually labeled based on what's inside:

- **Stock (Equity) Funds.** The most common. These boxes are filled with slices of companies. When you buy this box, you're betting on human productivity.

- **Bond (Fixed Income) Funds.** These boxes are filled with IOUs. You're basically lending your money to governments or big companies in exchange for a little "thank you" check (interest).
- **Mixed (Balanced) Funds.** These are the "surf and turf" of the fund world. They throw a bit of everything—stocks and bonds—into one box to try and smooth out the ride.
- **Commodity Funds.** Instead of companies, these boxes hold "stuff." Think gold, oil, or even wheat. You're betting on the price of raw materials.
- **Real Estate Funds.** These boxes let you own a "slice" of giant office buildings, malls, or apartment complexes without having to go out and fix a leaky toilet yourself.

Exchange Traded Funds (ETFs)

For a long time, the "Village Pool" (the Mutual Fund) had a bit of a bottleneck. Every time a villager wanted to put money in or take it out, they had to walk all the way to Mr. Smart's office. He had to stop what he was doing, count the cash, and issue a receipt. It was slow, clunky, and honestly, a bit of a hassle for everyone.

Then Mr. Smart had a better idea: **The Exchange-Traded Fund (ETF).**

Instead of everyone coming to his office, Mr. Smart listed the "Pool" on the town's big Stock Exchange. Now, instead of waiting a day for Mr. Smart to process a receipt, the villagers can just buy and sell their "slices" of the pool to each other in real time, right there on the exchange.

Here is why I think the villagers (and you) might like this better:

- **Speed.** You can buy or sell an ETF in seconds, just like a regular stock. You aren't stuck waiting for the end of the day to see what your price was.
- **Lower Costs.** Since Mr. Smart doesn't have to act like a bank teller anymore, he doesn't have to charge as much for administration. I've figured that ETFs are almost always cheaper to own than old-school mutual funds.
- **The "Magic" Price.** There is some complex math happening behind the curtain—done by big institutions—that ensures the price you pay on the exchange stays very close to the actual value of the "stuff" inside the bucket.

The Warning. I have to be honest with you: the "convenience" of an ETF is a double-edged sword. Because they are so easy to trade, it's tempting to jump in and out of them every time the news changes. Just because you *can* trade something every second doesn't mean you *should.* Don't let the speed turn you from a Marathoner into a panicked Sprinter.

US FUNDS BY THE NUMBERS

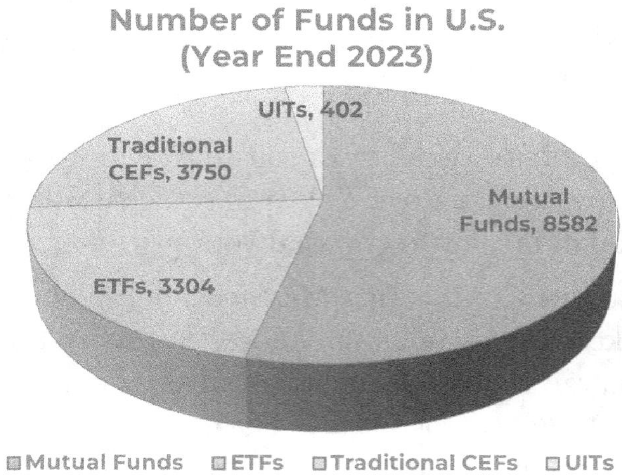

Total number of Funds: 16,038.
Source: 2024 Investment Company Factbook[44]

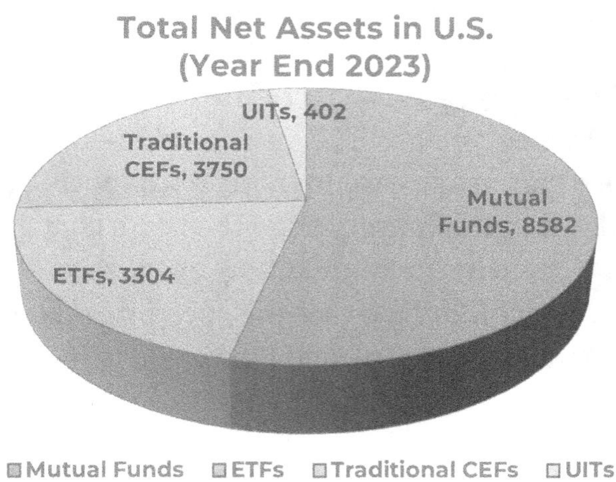

Total net assets (in billions): $33,930
Source: 2024 Investment Company Factbook[45]

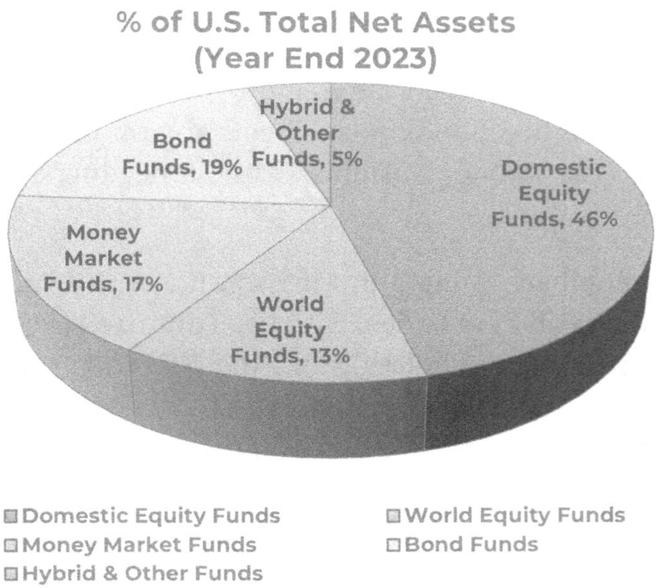

Source: 2024 Investment Company Factbook[46]

- **Home-Grown Stocks (Domestic)**: These funds buy shares in companies based right here in the U.S.
- **The World Tour (International)**: These funds loot to find companies in places like Europe or Asia.
- **The Waiting Room (Money Market)**: It's low-risk and designed for when you need to keep your money "on call."
- **The Mixed Bag (Hybrid & Alternatives):** These funds blend a bit of everything—stocks, bonds, and sometimes "stuff" like gold—into a single bucket.

SUMMARY: THE PROS AND CONS

In this chapter, we looked at handing the keys over to the professionals through Mutual Funds and ETFs. It's a step in the right direction because it gets you off the sidelines and into the "Money Machine" without needing a PhD in finance.

But remember: hiring a pro doesn't mean you can go to sleep. You still have to deal with the **Termites** (Fees), the **Maze** (too many choices), and the **Mirror** (your own emotions). Keep it in mind that while Mr. Smart (Chauffeur) can drive the bus, you're still the one who has to decide which bus to board and when to get off.

Let's Level for a Second. Just a final reminder: everything we talked about–the "Village Pool," Mr. Smart, and the different types of funds–is here to help you understand the landscape, not to tell you exactly where to put your money.

Investing in funds and ETFs involves real risk. Even the best "pros" lose money, and beating a benchmark doesn't guarantee a profit. Fees will eat into your gains, and the past is never a map for the future. Don't treat any of this as a "sure thing." Think for yourself, know your limits, and for the full legal details, see the disclaimer at the front of the book.

CHAPTER 6
PASSIVE INVESTING: THE "SMARTNESS" OF DUMB MONEY

In the last chapter, we looked at handing the keys to a pro like Mr. Smart. But once you're on the bus, how do you know if he's actually getting you anywhere? How do you tell if he's a superstar or just someone who's good at sounding smart while he sits in traffic?

To answer that, you need a **Scoreboard.** In the investing world, we call that an **Index.**

WHAT IS A STOCK MARKET INDEX?

An index is essentially a "fenced-in" group of stocks. It doesn't buy or sell anything; it just watches a specific group and tells you how they are doing as a team.

Think of it like a weather report for different parts of the economy. If the "Bank Index" is up but the "Transportation Index" is down, it means the bankers are having a great day while the truckers are stuck in the mud. It gives you a way to see who's winning and who's losing without having to check every single stock yourself.

THE WORLD'S BIGGEST SCOREBOARDS

- **S&P 500.** This is the big one. It tracks 500 of the biggest companies in the U.S. and acts as the "official score" for the entire American economy.
- **The Dow (DJIA).** An old-school list of 30 "Blue Chip" giants. It's like the Hall of Fame for American business.
- **Nasdaq Composite.** This is the tech-heavy scoreboard. If Silicon Valley is booming, this number is usually flying.
- **FTSE 100 (UK).** The top 100 heavyweights in London.
- **Nikkei 225 (Japan).** The main scoreboard for the biggest players in Tokyo.
- **Nifty 50 (India).** The 50 largest companies driving the Indian economy.

BUILDING MY OWN SCOREBOARD

To show you how this works, I decided to build my own "fake" index. I wanted to track how U.S. retailers were doing—companies like Walmart, Target, and Amazon. I called it the **"TDI Retail Index"** (The Dumb Investor Retail Index).

- **The Lineup.** I wanted a mix of everything—from where you buy your milk to where you order your gadgets. Here is who made the cut for the **TDI Retail Index**:

Company Name	What They Do
Walmart	Big-Box retailer
Amazon	The Online Everything Store

Company Name	What They Do
Costco	The Warehouse Club
Kroger	Your Neighborhood Grocer
The Home Depot	Home Improvement
CVS Health Corporation	Health and Pharmacy
TJX Companies	Apparel and Home Fashion (T.J. Maxx)

- **The "Price Tag" (Market Cap).** Before we can track the team, we need to know how big each player is. In the stock market, we call this **Market Capitalization**, think of it as the price tag for the entire company.

> **The Math.** If you wanted to buy every single share of a company and own it 100%, the "Price Tag" is:
> **The number of shares x The current stock price.**

I've done the math based on the prices from late 2025, and the results are staggering. It shows you just how lopsided the world can be:

Company Name	The Total Price Tag (Market Cap in $bn)
Walmart	897
Amazon	2440
Costco	377
Kroger	39
The Home Depot	345
CVS Health Corporation	99
TJX Companies	174
Total Team Value	4,371

Note: Market Data as of 12/22/2025. For illustrative purposes only and does not constitute financial advice.

- **The Starting Line.** Our "TDI Retail Team" has a total price tag of $4,371 billion. That's a massive, clunky number to track every day. To keep things simple, the industry uses a "Divisor"—basically a shrink-ray—to set the starting score to 100.

  Starting at 100 makes it incredibly easy to see how the team is doing at a glance. If the score goes to 105 tomorrow, the index is up 5%. If it drops to 95, it's down 5%. No calculators or complex math required.

- **The Lopsided Scorecard.** Now that we have our starting score of 100, we just watch the prices. But here's the "Dumb" secret of a market-cap index: **Not all players are equal.** Because Amazon is the 800-pound gorilla—making up nearly **50%** of our whole team—its "weight" pulls the scoreboard harder than anyone else. If Amazon has a bad day and trips, the whole team falls down, even if every other store on the list is having a great afternoon.

> **The Magnificent 7.** This is exactly how the real S&P 500 works. A handful of giants like Apple, Microsoft, and Nvidia (the "Magnificent 7") are so huge that they essentially drive the bus. If they decide to drive off a cliff, it doesn't matter if the other 493 companies are having a great day—the index is going down.

THE REAL-WORLD SCOREBOARD

If you looked at the official math for the S&P 500, you'd see a few more complications. It's okay to mostly ignore these, but you should know they exist:

- **Free-Float.** The pros don't count every single share of a company—only the ones that are actually "out in the wild" being traded. If a founder is hoarding 50% of the shares in a vault, those don't count toward the index score.
- **The Magic Divisor.** My simple math used a fixed number (43.71). In the real world, they tweak that number whenever a company does a "stock split" or pays a big dividend. It's their way of making sure the scoreboard doesn't jump around just because of some boring paperwork.

THE BIG THREE

While there are thousands of indices, these are the three "Scoreboards" you'll hear about every time you turn on the news.

S&P 500 INDEX (THE BIG PICTURE)

This is the heavyweight champion. It tracks 500 of the biggest companies in America. It's like a massive net that catches everything—from the "Magnificent 7" tech giants to the big banks (Chase), the oil companies (Exxon), and the stuff you use every day (Coke and McDonald's).

- **The Vibe.** If a company is a household name, it's probably in here.
- **The Weight.** Because it's "Market Cap Weighted," the giants carry more weight. This index represents about 80% of the value of the entire U.S. stock market. When

people ask, "How did the market do today?" this is the answer they're looking for.

THE NASDAQ COMPOSITE (THE TECH ENGINE)

Launched in 1971, this tracks over 2,500 stocks listed on the Nasdaq exchange. [47]

- **The Vibe.** It's the "cool kids" table. It's very heavy on technology and innovation.
- **The Weight.** Like the S&P, it's weighted by size. If tech is booming, the Nasdaq is flying; if tech is hurting, the Nasdaq usually feels the most pain.

THE DOW (THE OLD GUARD)

The Dow Jones Industrial Average is the "Grandpa" of the group, dating back to 1896. [48] It only tracks 30 massive, "Blue-Chip" companies.

- **The Vibe.** It's a very small, exclusive club.
- **The Quirky Bit.** Unlike the others, it's Price-Weighted. This means a company with a higher stock price has more influence than a company with a lower price, regardless of how big the company actually is.
- **The Reality.** It's a bit of a relic, and it doesn't cover nearly as much ground as the S&P 500, but because of its long history, people still watch it to see how the "Old Guard" of American industry is holding up.

S&P 500® VS NASDAQ COMPOSITE®

If you had to pick just one scoreboard to watch for the rest of your life, it would be the **S&P 500**. While the Nasdaq gets a lot of hype, the S&P 500 is the "Gold Standard" for a few very simple, common-sense reasons.

The Feature	S&P 500 (The All-American)	Nasdaq (The Tech-Specialist)
The Club	Admits the 500 biggest companies, regardless of which exchange they list on.	Tracks only Nasdaq companies. Ignores NYSE giants like Chase or Exxon.
The Variety	Provides a balanced meal: tech, banks, oil, healthcare, and retail.	Concentrates heavily on the "sugar": technology and innovation.
The Passport	Only allows U.S.-based companies in the index.	Includes foreign companies as well.
The Reach	The index represents 80% of the U.S. market capitalization.	Covers less ground, even though it has more names on the list.

The Dumb Take. If the Nasdaq is a specialized tree—built for a specific climate and capable of incredible things—then the S&P 500 is the **whole forest**. It's my personal favorite, and it's where I've chosen to park most of my life savings.

ACTIVE INVESTING: THE DELUXE BUS TICKET

Imagine you've got your retirement savings in a **Deluxe Bus**—a mutual fund—that charges a 1% fee. They tell you it's a "management fee," and on a small balance, it looks harmless. If you have $1,000 in there, you're paying $10 a year. That's a couple of coffees. No big deal, right?

But the "Money Machine" doesn't stay small forever. As your savings grow, those fees start to grow teeth.

- On **$100,000**, you're handing over **$1,000** every year.
- On **$500,000**, that's **$5,000** a year.

Think about that for a second. That is thousands of dollars leaving your pocket every single year, regardless of whether the **Chauffeur**—a fund manager—actually made you any money. Over a decade, you aren't just buying a few coffees; you're buying the manager a nice car.

THE "BEAT THE STREET" PROMISE

If you're paying that kind of money for a "pro" to drive the Deluxe Bus, you'd expect them to be better than the average driver. You're paying for a specialized skill.

The deal is simple:

- If the S&P 500 (the Scoreboard) goes up **4%**, you want your guy to hit **5%**.
- If the market crashes and drops **3%**, you want your guy to only drop **2%**.

In Wall Street lingo, this is called **"beating the street."** It's the idea that with enough research, enough coffee, and enough expensive suits, a human being can outsmart the collective wisdom of the entire market.

This hands-on, high-octane style of trying to pick the winners and dodge the losers is called **Active Investing**. It sounds great on a brochure, but let me tell you: in the real world, the "pros" rarely live up to the price tag.

THE TRUTH ABOUT THE "PROS"

If you're paying for a professional **Chauffeur**, you expect them to get you to your destination faster than the City Bus. You're paying for the shortcuts, the "inside track," and the expertise.

But when we look at the actual data—comparing those expensive **"Deluxe Buses"** (Active Funds) to the simple **"City Bus"** (the S&P 500)—the results are embarrassing. It turns out the City Bus is almost always faster, and it doesn't charge you a premium for the ride.

ACTIVE LARGE CAP DOMESTIC U.S. FUNDS VS S&P 500®

I looked at 23 years of data to see how often these high-paid managers (the "Active" guys) actually beat the "Dumb" S&P 500 index.

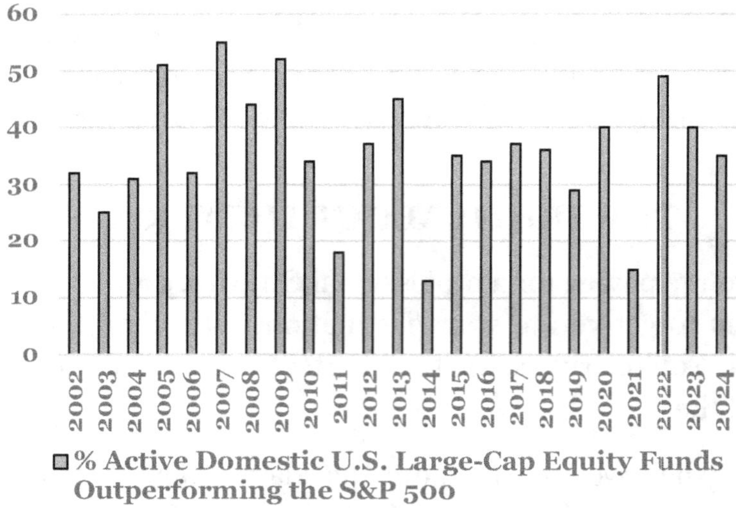

Source: S&P Dow Jones Indices, "SPIVA U.S. Year-End 2024 Scorecard" (2025).[49]

Reading the Scoreboard:

- **The Players:** "Active Domestic Large-Cap Funds" is just Wall Street speak for U.S. mutual funds run by pros who pick big-name stocks.
- **The Yardstick:** We use the S&P 500 because it's the heavyweight champion of big-company indices.
- **The Reality:** Every bar on this chart shows the percentage of "pros" who actually beat the index that year. Notice how the bars almost never cross the 50% line?

The Takeaway. In the last 23 years, there were only three years where more than half of the managers beat the scoreboard. Most of the time, the majority of the "geniuses" lost to a simple index.

THE HIDDEN GEM MYTH (MID AND SMALL CAPS)

You might be thinking, *"Okay, I get it. The S&P 500 is full of giants everyone knows about. But surely a pro can find some hidden winners in the medium-sized or smaller companies, right?"* It's a nice theory, but the scoreboard tells a different story. Whether you're looking at the **Mid-Cap** "middle children" or the **Small-Cap** "scrappy startups," the pros are still struggling to keep up with the simple indices.

THE MID-CAP SCOREBOARD (S&P 400)

These are the companies stuck in the middle—too big to be small, too small to be giants.

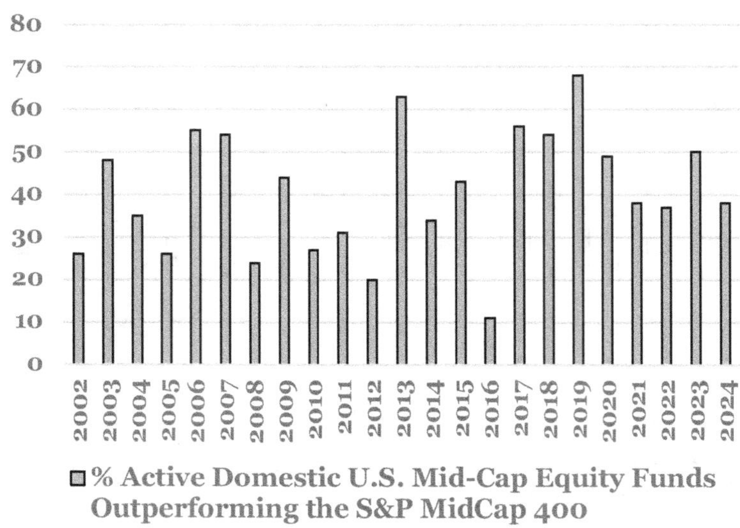

Source: S&P Dow Jones Indices, "SPIVA U.S. Year-End 2024 Scorecard" (2025).[50]

- **The Record:** In the last 23 years, there wasn't a **single year** where 75% of the "pro" managers beat the S&P MidCap 400 mid cap index.[51]
- **The 50/50 Toss-up:** Only **7 times out of 23** did at least half of the managers manage to outrun the index.
- **The Verdict:** Even in the "middle," the pros are mostly just expensive luggage.

THE SMALL-CAP SCOREBOARD (S&P 600)

This is where you'd expect the "research" to pay off. These are smaller companies where a "smart" manager should be able to find a diamond in the rough.

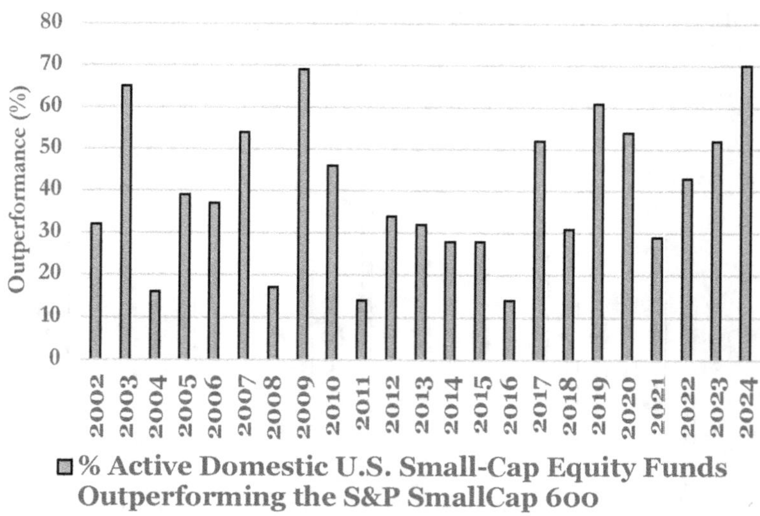

Source: S&P Dow Jones Indices, "SPIVA U.S. Year-End 2024 Scorecard" (2025).[52]

- **The Record:** Again, **zero years** out of 23 where 75% of the managers won.

- **The 50/50 Toss-up:** Only **8 years out of 23** did more than half of the managers beat the S&P SmallCap 600 small cap index.[53]
- **The Verdict:** The "scrappy startups" index is still beating the "experts" more than 60% of the time.

THE LONG RECORD: THE ODDS ARE STACKED AGAINST YOU

If you think the one-year stats were bad, look at what happens over the long haul. It turns out that while a "pro" might get lucky for a season, almost none of them can keep it up for decades.

Here is the percentage of professional managers who actually managed to beat the "Dumb" Scoreboard over time:

Fund Category	1Y (%)	5Y (%)	10Y (%)	20 Y (%)
Large-Caps (S&P 500)	~35%	~24%	~16%	~8.0%
Mid-Caps (S&P 400)	~38%	~20%	~23%	~9.1%
Small-Caps (S&P 600)	~70%	~40%	~18%	~9.2%

Source: S&P Dow Jones Indices, "SPIVA U.S. Year-End 2024 Scorecard" (2025).[54]

THE BRUTUAL REALTY

The "Vanishing Act." Notice how the numbers get smaller as the years go by? In the 20-year column, less than **10%** of the "experts" were able to beat a simple index. That means if you pick a professional manager today, there is a **90% chance** they will do worse than the index over the next two decades. Those are "Vegas" odds, and you're the one at the table.

It's Actually Worse Than It Looks. Here is the kicker: these performance numbers usually don't even include the "extra" hidden fees—the sales charges (entry/exit fees), the trading costs, and the taxes. Once you add those in, the "pro" performance drops even further into the basement.

The Impossible Choice. Wall Street wants you to believe you just need to find the "Top 10%" manager. But the way I see it, trying to pick that one superstar out of a crowd of thousands is like trying to find a needle in a haystack—while the haystack is on fire.

WELCOME TO PASSIVE INVESTING: THE LAZY WAY TO WIN

The numbers don't lie: the "Scoreboard" consistently beats the "Pros." And the longer you stay in the market, the more the index pulls ahead.

So, why not stop buying a **Deluxe Bus** ticket to try and outrun the traffic, and just hop on the **City Bus**? This strategy is called **Passive Investing**. Instead of paying a manager to guess which stocks will win, you simply buy the whole index and follow the proven route.

THE FATHER OF THE INDEX: JOHN C. BOGLE

While indices have been around for a long time, the idea of actually investing in them was considered crazy until the 1970s. That's when a man named John C. Bogle launched the first index fund for regular people like us (it's now the Vanguard 500).[55]

Bogle's big "aha!" moment was realizing that trying to beat the market is a **"loser's game."** Between the high fees and the human error, most people just end up poorer for trying. He famously told investors:

> **Don't look for the needle in the haystack. Just buy the haystack.**[56]

"TIME IS YOUR FRIEND; IMPULSE IS YOUR ENEMY"

Bogle knew that the hardest part of investing isn't the math—it's the mirror. He wanted investors to take a long-term view and ignore the screaming headlines and short-term "noise."

He even had a rule for when the market is crashing and everyone else is panicking: **"Don't do something, just stand there."**

The way I see it, most people are their own worst enemies. They sell when they're scared and buy when they're greedy. But the markets have a 100% track record of recovering and hitting new highs if you just give them enough time.

THE REVENGE OF THE "DUMB" INVESTOR

I've noticed a strange irony. The people who are "Dumb"—admitting they have little market knowledge but choosing to “Stay the Course”—are the ones who end up with the “magic” of a massive retirement account.

Meanwhile, the “so-called Smart” investors are often too busy fiddling, trading, and panicking to ever see those results. While they’re trying to outsmart the world, the “Dumb” investor is quietly winning by doing nothing.

HOW INDEX FUNDS WORK: THE MIRROR EFFECT

Remember our **TDI Retail Index** where Amazon was the 800-pound gorilla? An index fund for that index would simply go out and buy Amazon, Walmart, and the others in the exact same proportions.

The sole purpose of an index fund is to be a **mirror**. It isn't trying to be smarter than the index; it’s just trying to reflect it perfectly. If the index changes—say, a new company joins the club—the fund’s computers automatically swap the stocks to match.

Because there’s no high-priced “genius” in a suit spending all day researching and overthinking which stocks to buy, the whole thing runs on autopilot. That is why the fees are so low. You aren't paying for a brain; you’re paying for a very efficient mirror.

THE HEAD-TO-HEAD: ACTIVE VS. PASSIVE

Feature	Active Funds (The Deluxe Bus)	Passive Funds (The City Bus)
The Goal	Try to “Beat the Street.”	Simply match the scoreboard.

Feature	Active Funds (The Deluxe Bus)	Passive Funds (The City Bus)
The Style	Constant fiddling, guessing, and trading.	Hands-off. It only moves when the index moves.
The Cost	High. (0.5% – 2.0%+) You're paying for the driver's ego and research.	Tiny. (0.03% – 0.25%) You're just paying for a piece of software.
The Churn	High. Constant buying and selling (which costs you money in taxes).	Low. It rarely changes what it holds.
The Ego	High. The manager thinks they can dodge a crash.	Zero. It follows the rules, no matter what.

WHY IS IT HARD TO BEAT THE SCOREBOARD?

We've seen the data: outperforming the index is a brutal task. But why? If these managers are so smart and highly paid, why can't they just "pick the winners"? Here is the reality of what they are up against.

The Index is an "Automatic Winner" Machine. The S&P 500 is the ultimate "diversity" play. Because it holds 500 of the biggest players, it's virtually guaranteed to own every single winner in the large-cap world. But it's even smarter than that:

An Index automatically buys winners and sells losers

Because it's "Market Cap Weighted," as a company succeeds and grows, the Index automatically gives it more weight. If a company starts failing, the Index automatically shrinks its importance. It's a self-cleaning oven. While a human manager is overthinking whether to "hold or fold," the Index is already moving on to the next winner.

The "Fee" Weight Around Your Neck. Imagine two people running a race. One is wearing running shoes (The Index), and the other is carrying a 50-pound backpack full of expensive research reports and high-paid analysts (The Chauffeur).

Actively managed funds have to pay for fancy offices, "expert" salaries, and constant trading costs every time they buy or sell a stock. All those fees act like a lead weight. For a manager to even *tie* with the Index, they have to actually *outperform* it by 1% or 2% just to cover their own costs.

The "One-Hit Wonder" Problem. There are definitely talented managers who beat the market for a year or two. But as we saw in the long-term data, lightning rarely strikes twice—and almost never for twenty years straight. A "pro" might get lucky once, but trying to repeat that success over a lifetime is nearly impossible.

The Index Has No Heart (And That's a Good Thing). Investing is an emotional minefield. Humans are hardwired to panic when things go south and get greedy when things are booming. It's incredibly hard to "Stay the Course" when you're watching your life savings dip during a crash.

The Index, however, is a cold, calculated set of rules. It doesn't get scared. It doesn't get FOMO. It doesn't read the news and panic-sell at the bottom.

Fear and greed move people—but the index feels nothing

WHY THE "DUMB" ROUTE IS ACTUALLY SMARTER

Beating the index is a brutal task. While a few "Chauffeurs" manage to do it for a season or two, the odds of them doing it for a lifetime are slim. Here is why most investors are better off just sticking with the **City Bus**.

Picking a Winning Fund is Harder Than Picking a Stock. As I mentioned earlier, there are more mutual funds than there are companies on the stock exchange. Trying to rank them by their goals, fees, and track records is a full-time job in itself. By the time you find a "winner," the window of opportunity has often already closed.

Yesterday's Score Doesn't Predict Tomorrow's Win. Just because a team won the championship last year doesn't mean they'll win it this year. Fund managers use different "playbooks"—some are aggressive, some are defensive. No single playbook works in every kind of weather. As we saw in the data, while 23% of the pros beat the S&P 500 over five years, that number drops to a measly 8% over twenty years. Past performance is a shaky bridge to walk on.

The "Star" Manager Vanishing Act. When a manager becomes a "rockstar," they often leave their mutual fund to start a **Hedge Fund**. This is where things get really expensive. Hedge funds are essentially private clubs for the wealthy that use risky strategies and light oversight to try and "outsmart" the market.

The Hedge Fund Trap. These "exclusive" funds are famous for their "2 and 20" fee structure: they take **2%** of your money just for showing up and **20%** of any profit they make. That is a massive "lead weight" to carry. As far as I'm concerned you aren't missing out on anything. Historical data shows that once you account for those eye-watering fees, the "exclusive" wealth of the rich often grows slower than a simple, low-cost index fund available to everyone.

Individual Success Stories. We've all heard about the lucky few who got rich by getting into Apple or Nvidia early. It's tempting to call them geniuses, but to me, these stories are usually more about blind luck than brilliant analysis. For every person who caught lightning in a bottle, thousands of others "bet it all" on companies that no longer exist. You shouldn't confuse a lucky roll of the dice with a repeatable plan for your retirement.

> **A MILLION DOLLAR BET**
>
> To prove that the "Chauffeurs" weren't worth their high fees, Warren Buffett put his money where his mouth was. At the end of 2007, he bet one million dollars that a simple, low-cost S&P 500 index fund would outperform a group of elite hedge funds over ten years. [57]

The challenge was accepted by a pro who hand-picked five "funds of funds" (basically, a bus full of other chauffeurs). Buffett, on the other hand, just picked the **Vanguard 500 Index Fund** and went for a nap.

The bet ran from 2008 to 2017, and it wasn't even close. Buffett won in a landslide:

- **The "Dumb" Index:** Returned about **7.1%** a year.
- **The "Elite" Hedge Funds:** Managed only **2.2%** a year (after their massive fees).

THE ULTIMATE ADMISSION

When the bet ended, the pro who lost made a startling admission: he confessed that the high fees of hedge funds make it almost impossible to beat a low-cost index over time.

In my eyes, this is the most important lesson in this entire book. If the "smartest guys in the room" can't beat a simple, unmanaged index—even when there is a million dollars on the line—why would you pay them to try and do it with your retirement savings?

THE SMARTNESS OF DUMB MONEY

Based on everything we've looked at, the "Dumb" route isn't just a backup plan—it's usually the superior one. Warren Buffett, the greatest stock picker of all time, summed it up perfectly:

> **By periodically investing in an index fund, for example, the know-nothing**

> **investor can actually outperform most investment professionals. Paradoxically, when "dumb" money acknowledges its limitations, it ceases to be dumb** [58]

A NATIONAL WASTE OF TIME

Despite the overwhelming odds, millions of people still spend their nights and weekends obsessing over stock charts, watching "experts" on TV, and trading individual stocks.

My take is simple: This is a massive source of lost productivity and a national waste of time. Imagine if all that brainpower and energy were spent on people's actual jobs, their families, or their own businesses instead of trying to outsmart a computer in New York or Mumbai.

Both individuals and the economy would be much better off if people stopped trying to "play the market" every day. Instead, you should set your strategy, buy your "City Bus" ticket, and get back to living your life.

SUMMARY

In this chapter, we've unmasked the "**Scoreboard**" (the Index) and looked at the two ways professionals try to navigate the markets. While the "**Chauffeurs**" (Active Managers) promise the moon, the data shows they usually end up stuck in traffic.

Now, I'm not here to stop you if you really believe you can beat the system. If you choose the "Active" path and succeed, you are either exceptionally talented, incredibly lucky, or remarkably disciplined—usually all three. Just remember: don't celebrate too early. If you want to claim victory, you need to beat the Index for at least a decade, not just a weekend.

When you strip it all down, "**index funds**" are the ultimate gift of time. They offer you the growth of the entire world economy with minimal long-term risk. You aren't just buying a financial product; you're buying back your nights, your weekends, and your peace of mind.

The Fine Print. Before we move on, let's keep it real. This chapter is for **educational purposes** only—it isn't a personalized recommendation or investment advice.

Risk is inherent to the market. Investing in stocks or indices involves the very real chance of losing money. You can't "buy" an index directly (you buy the fund that follows it), and our **TDI Retail Index** is a hypothetical model, not a guarantee of future returns.

Fees still exist. While the "City Bus" is cheap, it still costs a little for gas and maintenance. Always check your own risk tolerance and financial situation before jumping in. For the full legal fine print, see the universal disclaimer at the front of the book.

CHAPTER 7
BONDS: THE FINE PRINT

In Chapter 2, we looked at Bonds as the "Boring but Reliable" sibling of the asset world. In this chapter, we're going to pop the hood and look at how they actually work. And honestly, the best way to understand a bond is to watch one live its entire life from birth to retirement.

LIFE OF A BOND

As we discussed earlier, **Treasuries** are just IOUs issued by the government. The "10-year Treasury" is the superstar of the bond world—it's the one everyone watches.

To keep things simple, let's follow a specific 10-year U.S. Treasury that was born in August 2019. Think of this as the "Birth Certificate" for our bond.

THE BIRTH (ISSUANCE)

Before we get into the nitty-gritty, let's look at the basic stats of this specific IOU.

Term	Value	What it actually means
Face Value	$1,000	The "Promise." This is the exact amount the government pays you back at the very end.
Interest Rate	1.625%	The "Rent." Since the government is borrowing your $1,000, they pay you

Term	Value	What it actually means
		$16.25 every year. They usually split this into two payments of $8.125.
Auction Date	Aug 7, 2019	The "Bidding War." This is when investors lined up to decide who gets to lend the government money.
Issue Date	Aug 15, 2019	The "Birthday." Investors handed over their cash, and the government handed over the IOU.
Maturity Date	Aug 15, 2029	The "Retirement." This is the day the deal ends. The government says "thanks," gives you your final interest, and returns your original $1,000.

THE LIFE (SECONDARY MARKET TRADING)

Trading of this bond began on its issue date, August 15, 2019. I should emphasize that **bond prices** fluctuate just like **stock prices**—a fact that surprises many investors. The primary driver of bond prices is **interest rates**. Let me show you how bond prices change based on interest rate movements.

Trading of this bond officially began on August 15, 2019. Now, here is the part that catches most people off guard: **Bond prices move up and down just like stocks.** Many people think a bond is a static piece of paper, but once it's out in the wild, its value changes every day. The biggest thing that moves that price? **Interest rates.** Think of it like a **See-Saw**. When interest rates in the world go up, the value of your "old" bond goes down. When rates go down, your bond becomes a hot commodity. Here is how that looked for our 2019 Treasury:

Scenario 1: Rates Drop (July 2020). By mid-2020, the world had changed, and new bonds were only paying about **0.65%**. Suddenly, your "old" bond paying **1.625%** looked like a golden ticket. Because your "rent" was higher than what anyone else could get, investors were willing to pay a **premium** to take it off your hands. Your $1,000 bond was suddenly worth about **$1,094**.

Scenario 2: The Sweet Spot (November 2021). For a brief moment, the rest of the world caught up to you. Market rates were right around **1.625%**. Since your bond wasn't any better or worse than a new one, it traded at **"Par"**—meaning it was worth almost exactly its **$1,000** face value.

Scenario 3: Rates Skyrocket (October 2023). This is where it gets painful. By late 2023, new bonds were paying a whopping **4.45%**. Why would anyone want your measly **1.625%** bond when they could get way more elsewhere? To sell it, you'd have to offer a massive **discount**. Your $1,000 bond's value crashed to around **$774**.

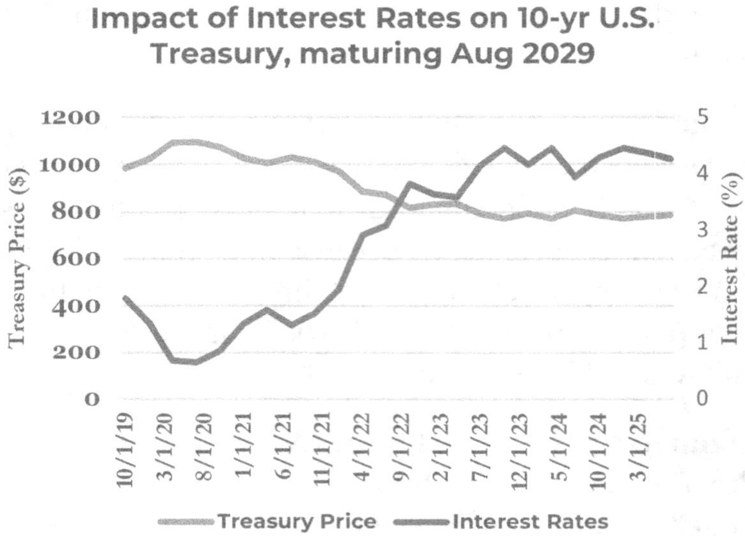

Source: Federal Reserve Bank of St. Louis (FRED), "10-Year Treasury Constant Maturity Rate" (2025).[59]

Note: Treasury prices were calculated using FRED 10-year constant-maturity yields and are intended to provide a close approximation. Actual prices may vary depending on market conditions

THE BOND SEE-SAW

The scenarios we've looked at all point to one golden rule: bond prices and interest rates are on a **See-Saw**.

When interest rates rise, bond prices fall. If new bonds pay more than yours, your "old" bond is worth less.

When interest rates fall, bond prices rise. If your bond pays more than the new ones, it becomes a "Golden Ticket" and people will pay a premium to own it.

THE DEATH (MATURITY)

No matter how much the price wiggles during its life, every bond eventually reaches its "expiration date." On **August 15, 2029**, our Treasury officially retires. When that clock hits zero, three things happen:

You get your "Promise" back. The U.S. government sends you the full **$1,000 face value**, regardless of whether the bond was trading for $700 or $1,100 the week before.

The final "Rent" check. You get one last interest payment of **$8.125**.

Game Over. The bond vanishes. It stops earning interest, it disappears from the trading floor, and it's officially "paid in full."

CREDIT QUALITY: THE "TRUST" FACTOR

A bond is only as good as the person promising to pay you back. While the government or a massive corporation might "promise" to return your cash with interest, there is always a chance they could trip up and **default**—meaning they simply don't pay. This risk is called **Credit Quality**, and it's the secret ingredient that determines a bond's price.

To help you judge who is a safe bet and who is a gamble, professional "referees" like **Moody's, S&P, and Fitch** give every bond a grade. These ratings tell you how likely it is that you'll actually see your money again.

THE CREDIT RATINGS DIVIDE

Wall Street loves its alphabet soup, but all those letters basically tell you one thing: how much sleep you're going to lose. While different rating agencies use slightly different codes, they all fall into three main buckets of risk.

High-Quality (The "Gold Standard"). Rated **AAA to A**. These are the "Bulletproof" bonds. They are the safest place to park your cash and should be the bedrock of your medium-term strategy. You won't get rich off the interest, but you can be almost certain the money will be there when you need it.

Lower Investment Grade (The "Fair Weather" Bonds). Rated **BBB or Baa**. Regulators still call these "safe," but they are much more sensitive to the economy. If a nasty recession hits, these are the bonds most likely to be downgraded or start shaking. They pay a bit more "rent," but they come with a side of anxiety.

Non-Investment Grade (The "Junk" Pile). Rated **BB+ or Ba1 and below**. These carry a significantly higher risk of default and are famously known as **Junk Bonds**. Don't let the word "Bond" fool you into thinking you're safe; when the stock market crashes, these often crash right along with it. They aren't "boring" safety nets; they are high-risk bets.

THE COST OF "SHAKY" PROMISE

Imagine two identical bonds. Both pay the same "rent" and both promise to pay you back in ten years. But one is from the **U.S. Government** and the other is from a **struggling tech startup**.

The Gold Standard (AAA). The U.S. Treasury is the "Safest Bet" on the planet. Because everyone trusts the government to pay them back, the demand is huge. Since it's so safe, the government doesn't have to work hard to find buyers—which means they can offer a **lower yield**.

The Risky Bet (BBB). The corporation, on the other hand, is subject to the whims of the economy. There's a real chance they could go bust. To get you to part with your cash, they have to "bribe" you with a **higher yield**. You're getting paid extra for the stress of wondering if they'll still be around in a decade.

Issuer	S&P Rating	The Vibe	Implication
U.S. Gov	AAA	Bulletproof.	Very safe, but you'll get a lower "rent" check.
Corporation	BBB	Decent, but watch out.	Higher risk of default means they pay you more to stay.

THE MYTH OF THE "SAFE" BOND

Many people buy bonds because they want to sleep at night, but I need to be clear: **Bonds can crash, too.** If the person who borrowed your money starts looking like they can't pay it back, the value of that IOU will fall off a cliff.

The Lehman and Enron Lessons. During the 2008 financial crisis, Lehman Brothers collapsed, and their bonds—once considered solid—plummeted to just **9 cents on the dollar**.[60] Similarly, when Enron's accounting scandal came to light, their bondholders were left fighting for pennies.[61] In both cases, people who thought they were "safe" lost almost everything and spent years in court trying to get a fraction of their money back.

Ratings Are Not a Guarantee. A high credit rating is just an "expert's" best guess. It's a "good-faith" grade, not a promise from God. Both Lehman and Enron were rated as "Investment Grade" (safe) almost right up until the day they died. I would say, a rating is a useful tool, but you should never follow it blindly.

THE TRUTH ABOUT YIELD

Now that we know the price moves, we look at the math of the "deal."

STICKER PRICE VS. REALITY.

Before we look at what moves a bond's price, we need to understand a word Wall Street loves to throw around: **Yield.** While "Interest Rate" is fixed on the day the bond is born, "Yield" is what you actually earn based on the price you paid for the ticket.

Current Yield. This is simply the "Rent" check divided by the price you paid for the bond. For example, if you buy a $1,000 bond for a discount price of **$900**, and it pays you **$50** a year in interest, your Current Yield is **5.55%** ($50 / $900).

Yield to Maturity (YTM). This is the "Total Ride" return. It counts the annual rent checks *plus* the extra cash you make (or lose) when the bond dies and pays you back the full **$1,000**. If you bought that bond for **$900**, your YTM is higher than the interest rate because you're also getting a **$100 bonus** at the end.

The Difference. Plain and Simple, the "Interest Rate" is the sticker price, but the "Yield" is the reality. Yield uses your actual purchase price, not the $1,000 written on the bond's birth certificate.

THE "TIME" FACTOR: WHY LONG BONDS WIGGLE MORE

There is one other rule to the Bond See-Saw: **The longer the bond has left to live, the more its price swings.**

The "Locked-In" Trap. If you have a 30-year bond, you are "locked in" to that interest rate for three decades. If rates go up next year, your bond looks terrible for a long, long time. But if you have a 2-year bond, the finish line is right there. Because you'll get your full $1,000 back very soon, the price doesn't need to swing as wildly.

The Gravity of Maturity. As a bond gets closer to its "death" date, the price naturally drifts back toward the **$1,000 Face Value**. Why? Because there are fewer "rent" checks left to worry about. The "See-Saw" loses its power as the finish line gets closer.

HOW SAFE ARE BONDS?

Now that we know how the plumbing works, we have to ask the big question: how safe is your money? When you buy a bond, you're basically managing two different kinds of "danger zones."

The Danger Zone	Top-Rated Bond Fund (The Bus)	Buying Directly (The IOU)
The "Rent" *(Interest Risk)*	**Very Low.** One bad apple won't spoil the bunch. If one company misses a payment, the other hundreds in the fund keep the checks coming.	**Gold Standard.** U.S. Treasuries are backed by the govt. Corporate bonds are a close second, but you're trusting a board of directors, not a country.
The "Pile" *(Principal Risk)*	**Wiggles Daily.** The fund's price (NAV) moves with the See-Saw. If rates spike and you need to sell during a "market tantrum," your pile might be smaller than it started.	**Depends on the "Fuse."** Short-term bonds are rock-solid. Long-term bonds (10yr+) swing wildly with interest rates if you try to sell them early.
The "Trap" *(Opportunity Risk)*	**Less Sticky.** Because funds constantly buy new bonds, they adjust to higher rates faster than a single locked-in bond.	**The Locked-In Blues.** If you hold to the end, you get your $1,000 back, but you might be stuck with a low "rent" while the rest of the world earns more.
The "Trust" *(Default Risk)*	**Buffered.** Diversification protects you from a single collapse. It's rare for a whole fund of top-tier bonds to vanish.	**Individual Exposure.** If you stray from Uncle Sam to a corporation that goes bust, your "Pile" could disappear entirely. No safety net here.

WHEN THE "SAFE HAVEN" GETS BUMPY

We're told that U.S. Treasuries are the safest bet in the world, and in terms of getting your money back, they are. But as the table below shows, their *price* can still take you for a wild ride.

Year	Return	The Vibe	What Happened
1982	32.81%	The Great Rally	Inflation finally calmed down, and bond prices went through the roof. It was one of the best years ever to own an IOU.
1994	-8.04%	The Bond Massacre	The Fed hiked interest rates to stop inflation, and bondholders got crushed as the "See-Saw" tipped the wrong way.
2008	20.10%	The Panic to Safety.	As the world economy melted down, everyone ran to Treasuries for cover, driving prices way up.
2009	-11.12%	The Morning After.	As the 2008 panic eased, people got brave again and sold their "safe" bonds to buy stocks, causing prices to dip.
2020	11.33%	The Pandemic Surge.	COVID-19 sent everyone back into "safety mode," and the Fed dropped rates to zero to keep the lights on.
2022	-17.83%	The Inflation Shock.	To fight rising prices, the Fed hiked rates faster than we'd seen in decades. It was the worst year for bonds in modern history.

Source: Damodaran (1928-2024) and Federal Reserve Economic Data (FRED). For full details, see End Notes. [62]

TIMING THE BOND

In his classic book, *The Intelligent Investor*, Benjamin Graham gives a blunt warning to anyone trying to outsmart the market:

> **If it is virtually impossible to make worthwhile predictions about the price movements of stocks, it is completely impossible to do so for bonds**[63]

I suggest you take this warning to heart. Trying to guess which way interest rates will move is a game even the pros lose.

SUMMARY

In this chapter, we've looked at how the bond market actually works and why those prices move. Wall Street loves to use comforting labels like **"Fixed Income," "Capital Preservation,"** and **"Risk-Free."** While those terms are mostly true for things like U.S. Treasuries–where the government is almost certain to pay you back–you can still get burned. I've seen it happen before–the "See-Saw" tips the wrong way and people are forced to sell early.

Bonds might be the "boring" sibling of the stock market, but don't mistake boring for "bulletproof." They are less volatile than stocks, but they aren't a guaranteed safe harbor if you don't respect the risks

A Word of Caution: This chapter is here to show you how the plumbing works, not to tell you exactly which bond to buy today. The history we've looked at—from the **"See-Saw"** to the **2022 "Bond Massacre"**—is meant to illustrate the risks, not to predict the future.

Every person's **"Pile"** and timeline are different. Investing in bonds involves real risk, and history isn't a crystal ball. **Plain and simple**, what worked in 1982 might not work in 2026. Before you make any moves with your own money, be sure to check the universal disclaimer at the start of this book for the full legal details.

CHAPTER 8 PUTTING THE PIECES TOGETHER

We've spent the last seven chapters gathering the ingredients; now it's time to actually cook the meal. Before we throw everything into the pan, let's take a quick look at the "Dumb Investor" toolkit we've built so far.

The Foundation (The 4Qs). We started by stripping away the jargon and asking the only four questions that actually matter: **Where, When, How Much,** and **How Long?** We anchored these in common sense—managing risk, keeping things liquid, and keeping our emotions on a short leash.

The Building Blocks. We looked at the "Big Five" of the investment world: **Equities, Bonds, Real Estate, Commodities,** and **Cash.** We didn't just look at the textbook definitions; we looked at their history and their "personalities" to see how they behave when the market gets moody.

The Strategy (Index vs. The Pros). We pulled back the curtain on Wall Street and saw that most of the "experts" are just expensive guesses. We discovered that for most of us, **Passive Indexing**—staying simple and keeping costs low—is the most reliable way to actually keep more of your money.

The Anchor (Bonds). Finally, we mastered the **Bond See-Saw**. We learned that while bonds are the "boring" part of the portfolio, they are essential for stability—provided you respect the "Trust Factor" and the "Time Fuse."

WAYS TO MANAGE THE "PILE"

Now that you have the ingredients, we need to decide how to run the kitchen. There are a few different ways to organize your money, and each one helps you answer your **4Qs** without getting overwhelmed by the noise of the market.

STRATEGIC ASSET ALLOCATION (SAA) (THE "FIXED RECEIPE" APPROACH")

SAA is the most common way people manage their money.[64] You'll find it in every textbook and every online calculator. The idea is simple: you pick a "fixed recipe" (a percentage) for your stocks, bonds, and cash, and you stick to it.

How it works. You decide on a mix that fits your gut for risk and your timeline.

- **The "Gas" (80% Stocks / 20% Bonds):** If you have decades before you need the cash, you lean heavily on stocks to grow your pile.
- **The "Brakes" (60% Stocks / 40% Bonds):** If you're closer to needing the money or you just hate seeing big swings, you add more bonds to steady the ride.

Rebalancing (Cleaning the Kitchen). Over time, the market will mess up your recipe. If stocks have a great year, your "80% stocks" might drift up to 85%. SAA requires you to "rebalance"—selling a bit of stocks and buying a bit of bonds—to get back to your original mix.

Why people love it. It's simple, disciplined, operating on a pre-set maintenance schedule. Instead of wondering "What should I do today?", you just look at your recipe. It's the "Gold Standard" for anyone managing their own retirement accounts (IRAs) or brokerage accounts.

TARGET DATE FUND (TDF)—THE "AUTO-PILOT" GLIDE PATH

Target Date Funds are the ultimate "set-it-and-forget-it" tool.[65] They are the most popular way to invest globally because they do the heavy lifting for you. You simply pick a year that matches your goal—like retirement in 2050 or a kid starting college in 2035—and the fund takes over the steering wheel.

The Glide Path. When the date is far away, the fund is aggressive, holding mostly stocks to grow your "Pile." As you get closer to the finish line, the fund automatically shifts into "safety mode," selling stocks and buying more bonds and cash. It "glides" from growth to protection without you having to lift a finger.

The Default Choice. In the U.S., if you have a **401(k)** at work and haven't picked your own investments, there is a very good chance your money is already in one of these.

It's the largest investment framework in the world because it's the easiest.

THREE BUCKET STRATEGY (THE "MENTAL PEACE" APPROACH)

While the other strategies focus on percentages, this one focuses on **Time**. You organize your money into three distinct buckets based on when you actually need to spend it. [66] Think of it like stocking a kitchen: you have the stuff you need for dinner tonight, the stuff you keep in the pantry for next month, and the stuff you're aging in the cellar for the long haul.

The "Now" Bucket (0–3 Years: The Fridge)

This is your **"Spending"** bucket. You don't put things in the fridge to keep them for a decade; you put them there because you're hungry now. You need the contents to be fresh, safe, and ready to grab.

- **What goes in here:** The **"Monthly Nut"** (bills/groceries), your **"Life Happens"** fund (emergencies), and any **"Upcoming Milestones"** (a vacation or car down payment) within the next three years.
- **The Mission: Zero Surprises.** You need to know that if you reach into this bucket, $100 is still $100. This money stays in a "safe room" where the value doesn't wiggle and the door is always unlocked. It isn't there to grow; it's there to be ready.

The "Soon" Bucket (4–8 Years: The Pantry)

This is the **"Bridge"** bucket. Like a pantry, these are things you'll need "soon," but not tonight. It's for mid-range goals that aren't immediate but aren't thirty years away, either.

- **What goes in here: "Mid-Range Goals"** like a house down payment in five years or a kid starting college in six. It also acts as your **"Safety Net"**—if the market stays down for a long time and your fridge runs dry, you pull from the pantry instead of raiding your long-term wealth.
- **The Mission: Beating Inflation.** This bucket can handle a little bit of "wobble." We want it to grow faster than a savings account, but we aren't swinging for the fences. It's about keeping your purchasing power alive without taking on too much drama.

The "Later" Bucket (9+ Years: The Cellar)

This is the **"Engine"** of your wealth. Think of this like a wine cellar or a root cellar. This is for the stuff that takes a long time to mature—retirement, a legacy, or big dreams way down the road.

- **The Mission: Pure Growth.** Because you don't need this money to pay for next year's groceries, you can lock the cellar door and let it out into the wild. The goal is to let your money work for you, using the power of **Compounding** to turn a small "Pile" into a mountain over the decades.
- **Risk Profile: The Long View.** This bucket will have the most "wobble." It will go up and it will go down.

But because your timeline is measured in decades, the short-term drama doesn't matter. You are using **Time as a shield** to ignore the market's bad moods.

HOW THEY STACK UP?

Wall Street has a million ways to slice the pie, but for most of us, it comes down to these three paths. Here is how they actually compare when you put them side-by-side.

Feature	Strategic Allocation	Target-Date Fund (TDF)	Three-Bucket Strategy
The Core Idea	**The Fixed Recipe.** You pick a % (like 60/40) and stick to it.	**The Auto-Pilot.** The fund shifts from "Growth" to "Safety" as you age.	**The Time Zones.** You divide money by when you actually need to spend it.
Management	**Hands-On.** You have to rebalance it yourself when things drift.	**Hands-Off.** The computer handles the shifts and the rebalancing.	**Active Flow.** You rearrange money into the three buckets as your needs change.
The Vibe	Disciplined, but can be stressful when the market tanks.	Simple and mindless. Great for "forgetting" about your 401(k).	**Peace of Mind.** Knowing your next 3 years of bills are paid stops the panic.
Custom Fit	**Tailor Made.** You build it exactly to your own risk level.	**One-Size-Fits-All.** Everyone retiring in 2050 gets the same mix, regardless of their health, wealth, or other income.	**Ultra-Personal.** You decide exactly how big each bucket needs to be.

Feature	Strategic Allocation	Target-Date Fund (TDF)	Three-Bucket Strategy
Spending Plan	You usually follow a math rule (like the "4% Rule") to take money out.	The fund gets safer, but you still need a plan for the actual withdrawals.	**Built-In.** The first bucket is your spending plan. It's ready when you are.

Why The Three-Bucket Strategy Wins

Among the three paths we've walked, the **Three-Bucket Strategy** is the one that actually lives in the real world. Here's why it's the primary tool we're going to use for the rest of this book.

TDFs are too "Generic." Target-date funds assume every 40-year-old has the same "Pile" and will retire on the exact same Tuesday. But a millionaire with a pension can take risks that someone scraping by can't, and neither of them knows for sure when life will actually force them to retire. The computer follows a fixed calendar—but your buckets follow your life.

SAA is just "Guessing with Math." Picking a percentage like 60/40 or 70/30 feels precise, but to me it's often just an arbitrary guess. Does a 10% difference in bonds really change how you pay your mortgage next month? Probably not. SAA is a label; Buckets are a plan.

It's a Shield for Your Brain. Watching a $1,000,000 portfolio drop to $750,000 is gut-wrenching, especially if you have to sell stocks while they're "on sale" just to buy groceries. This is how people panic and make permanent mistakes. With buckets, you know your spending money is tucked away in a safe spot, allowing you to ignore the market's "tantrums" in your growth pile.

It Protects Against "Bad Timing." There is a technical nightmare called **Sequence-of-Returns Risk**. It's just a fancy way of saying "the market crashed right when I retired." If you're using a traditional percentage mix, you might be forced to sell your stocks at the absolute bottom just to keep the lights on. The Three-Bucket Strategy is a mechanical shield—you spend from the "Safe" bucket and give the "Growth" bucket the time it needs to heal.

Because of these strengths, I will use the Three-Bucket Strategy as our primary framework for the rest of this book.

WHERE SHOULD I INVEST?

Knowing the theory is one thing; actually "stocking" the buckets is where the rubber meets the road. To do this right, we have to match the right investment "tool" to the right time frame.

The "Now" Bucket (0–3 Years)

For your **Fridge**, we only care about two things: **Safety** and **Speed**.

Looking back at our menu of assets—stocks, bonds, real estate, and commodities—there is only one that belongs here: **Cash.**

Why Cash is King Here You can't pay your mortgage with a "potential" gain in the stock market or a piece of a rental property. You need dollars that don't wiggle. Cash and its close cousins are the only assets where $100 stays $100, no matter what the headlines say. It's about preserving your pile and being able to grab it the second life happens.

A Sample "Now" Setup

The Asset	How Much?	The Job Description
Checking Account	1–2 months of Bills	The "Monthly Nut." Immediate cash for groceries, gas, and rent.
High-Yield Savings (HYSA)	The Rest of Bucket 1	The "Back-up." Safe, easy to reach, and earns a bit of "rent" (interest).

- **High-Yield Savings (HYSA):** These are usually at online banks. They pay much more than the big "brick-and-mortar" banks, but remember: the interest rates are variable. They move up and down based on what the Federal Reserve decides.
- **The CD Sidekick:** A **Certificate of Deposit (CD)** can work well here. A 3-month CD might pay more than a savings account, but you're "locking" your money in a vault. If you need it early, the bank hits you with a penalty. It's a solid move if you're certain you won't need that specific chunk of cash for a few months.
- **What I Leave Out:** I don't bother with **Treasury bills** or **corporate paper** here. While they're safe, the extra hoop-jumping and paperwork usually aren't

worth the tiny bit of extra interest. For most of us, a good HYSA does 99% of the job with 0% of the headache.

The "Soon" Bucket (4–8 Years: The Pantry)

For the **Pantry**, we need assets that can beat inflation without the "heart-attack" volatility of the stock market. This is the "bridge" between your daily spending and your long-term wealth.

The Asset of Choice: High-Quality Bonds. Bonds are the middle ground. They usually pay better "rent" than a savings account, but they are much more stable than stocks.

A Sample "Soon" Setup

The Asset	How Much?	The Job Description
Medium-Term Bond Fund	100% of Bucket 2	A buffer for mid-range goals and a backup for your "Now" bucket.

- **Why a Fund?** I suggest using a bond fund rather than buying individual bonds. It's a "hands-off" way to get a professional mix of high-quality debt without the extra paperwork.
- **The Maturity Match:** We stick to funds holding bonds that mature in that 4–8 year window. Going "longer" adds too much price-swinging drama for this bucket.

The "Later" Bucket (9+ Years: The Cellar)

This is the **Cellar**, the "Engine Room" of your wealth. Since we aren't touching this for a decade or more, we can finally stop playing it safe and go for **Pure Growth**.

The Asset of Choice: Equities (Stocks) Based on the history we looked at in Chapter 3, nothing builds wealth quite like the stock market over the long haul.

A Sample "Later" Setup

The Asset	How Much?	The Job Description
S&P 500 Index Fund	100% of Bucket 3	Growing your "Pile" through the power of compounding.

- **Low-Cost Indexing:** As we covered in Chapter 6, don't try to pick individual "winners." A low-cost S&P 500 fund gives you a piece of the 500 biggest companies in America. It's cheap, effective, and beats the "pros" most of the time.
- **What I Leave Out (Gold):** You'll notice there is no gold here. While gold has its moments, my aim is to keep things simple and avoid overcomplication. We're building a wealth engine, not a jewelry box.

HOW MUCH SHOULD I INVEST?

Once you know where the money goes, the next question is: *How much goes into each unit?* There is no magic formula because your life isn't a math problem. The size of your buckets depends on your age, your health, and how much "wiggle room" you need to sleep at night. While I'll give you specific sample setups in the next two chapters, here is the common-sense way to start.

PRIORITIZE SAFETY (PLAN THE FRIDGE AND PANTRY FIRST)

Your first job is to make sure you can eat today and keep the lights on tomorrow. You shouldn't be swinging for the fences in the **"Cellar" (Long-Term)** until you have a solid plan for your **"Fridge"** and **"Pantry."** Depending upon your situation, it might be perfectly okay to start contributing to the **Cellar** early, provided you aren't leaving the **Fridge** bone-dry.

THE "LATER" BUCKET IS THE OVERFLOW

Once you've decided how much cash and bonds you need to feel secure for the next eight years, the calculation for your Long-Term bucket becomes easy: **It's whatever is left over. Keep it simple:** Any dollar that isn't spoken for by your short- or medium-term needs belongs in the growth engine.

- **Don't overextend:** Never put money in the "Cellar" that you might need to buy a car next year. Forcing yourself to sell stocks during a market "tantrum" because you ran out of grocery money is how permanent mistakes happen.

CONSISTENCY OVER PERFECTION

Don't wait for a "perfect" plan or a giant inheritance to start. The secret isn't how much you start with; it's the rhythm you keep. A steady stream of small contributions will beat a "perfectly timed" lump sum almost every time.

HOW LONG SHOULD I INVEST?

The question of "how long" is actually built into the structure of the buckets. Instead of guessing when to sell or how long to wait, the strategy tells you exactly when to move. Each bucket has a job based on its expiration date, which determines its timeline.

THE FRIDGE (0–3 YEARS)

This money is already "at the table." Because you need it for bills and immediate milestones, you aren't waiting for a market cycle to finish. You spend it as life happens.

THE PANTRY (4–8 YEARS)

This money is "on deck." It stays invested in stable assets (like bonds) long enough to beat inflation, but its ultimate job is to refill the Fridge. When your short-term cash starts to run low, you tap into the Pantry to keep your immediate needs covered.

THE CELLAR (9+ YEARS)

This is the only bucket where "How long?" has an absolute answer: As long as possible. This money is the engine of your wealth. Unless there is a total emergency that empties your first two buckets, you leave the Cellar door locked. You give these investments the decades they need to grow and compound without interruption.

THE TAKEAWAY

The bucket strategy takes the guesswork out of selling. You don't sell your long-term stocks because the news is bad; you only move money when a bucket's "time is up" and it needs to move to the next unit. By dividing your money this way, you stop being a market-timer and start being a manager of your own timeline.

WHEN SHOULD I INVEST

The short answer is: **Yesterday.** But for most of us, the fear of "buying at the top" is enough to keep our money sitting on the sidelines for years. To fix this, we use a strategy that takes the brain—and the ego—out of the equation.

DOLLAR COST AVERAGING (DCA)

Trying to time the market is a fool's errand. Even the pros, with their supercomputers and Ivy League degrees, rarely get it right. Decades ago, Benjamin Graham (the mentor to Warren Buffett) popularized a much simpler path: instead of trying to buy at the absolute low or sell at the high, you just keep buying, no matter what.

By spreading your investments over time, you effectively "average out" the price you pay. You stop worrying about whether the market is "expensive" today because you know you'll be buying again next month when it might be "on sale."[67]

The "Set-It-And-Forget-It" Plan

Imagine you have $1,000 to invest every month. You could spend hours analyzing charts and reading headlines, trying to find the perfect Tuesday to jump in. Or, you could set up a **Systematic Investment Plan (SIP)**.

An SIP is an automated tool that pulls that $1,000 from your bank account and puts it to work on the same day every month, rain or shine.

- **When the market is up:** Your $1,000 buys fewer shares, but your existing pile is worth more.
- **When the market is down:** Your $1,000 buys *more* shares. You are essentially "stocking up" while prices are low.

DCA In Action

To see how this works in the real world, look at what happens over a year when you commit to that $1,000 monthly drip into an **S&P 500 Index Fund**, regardless of the price.

Month	Price Per Unit	Units Bought
Jan	$50	20.00
Feb	$48	20.83
Mar	$52	19.23

Month	Price Per Unit	Units Bought
Apr	$47	21.28
May	$49	20.41
Jun	$51	19.61
Jul	$50	20.00
Aug	$53	18.87
Sep	$55	18.18
Oct	$52	19.23
Nov	$50	20.00
Dec	$48	20.83
Total	$12,000 Invested	238.47 Units

Average Cost per Unit: $50.36

This approach saves you from the emotional rollercoaster of second-guessing yourself. You aren't gambling on a moment; you are betting on a timeline.

THE POWER OF AUTOMATIC

The beauty of this chart isn't the math—it's the **behavior**. When the price dropped to $47 in April, you didn't panic; your automatic plan simply bought you more units. When it spiked to $55 in September, you didn't get greedy; you just bought a little less.

While we usually talk about this for the **Cellar** (Stocks), the rule of "consistency over perfection" applies to the whole house. If your **Fridge** or **Pantry** are looking a little empty, the answer is the same: don't wait for a windfall. Just start a steady drip of funds.

The goal is to remove the emotional stress of "when" by making the "when" automatic.

THE CORE LESSON

By taking the "when" out of your hands, you gain three massive tactical advantages:

- **Timing is a myth:** DCA kills the need to be a psychic.
- **Pressure is gone:** You don't have to pick the "perfect" Tuesday to buy.
- **Emotions are sidelined:** You stop checking the ticker because the machine is doing the work for you.

THE THREE BUCKET STRATEGY SUMMARY

Feature	Short Term (The Fridge)	Medium Term (The Pantry)	Long Term (The Cellar)
The Goal	Immediate Spending	The "Bridge"	Wealth Engine
Asset Class	Cash & Equivalents	High-Quality Bonds	Equities (Stocks)
Amount	0–3 Years of Expenses	Next 5 Years of Expenses	The "Overflow" (The Rest)
Timeline	0–3 Years	4–8 Years	9+ Years
The Focus	Safety & Liquidity	Beating Inflation	Pure Growth
Risk Level	Minimal	Low to Moderate	High (Short-term)

SUMMARY

We've now answered the "4Qs" of investing—**Where, When, How Much, and How Long**—using the Three-Bucket Strategy.

This framework isn't just a set of rules; it's a living version of the Core Principles we covered at the start of this book. Each bucket has a specific job to do in your financial house:

- **The Fridge (Short-Term):** Prioritizes safety and liquidity. It's your fortress against the unexpected.
- **The Pantry (Medium-Term):** Balances stability with a bit of growth to keep you ahead of inflation.
- **The Cellar (Long-Term):** Focuses on pure growth and the power of compounding.
- **The Clock (DCA):** Dollar Cost Averaging keeps you disciplined, making your investments automatic so your emotions don't get in the driver's seat.

By matching your assets to your timeline, the 4Qs become much easier to navigate. You no longer have to guess when to buy, how long to wait, or when it's safe to spend. You aren't just "investing"; you are managing a system designed for mental peace.

The final piece of the puzzle is determining the exact dollar amounts that should go into each bucket. We'll dive into those specific numbers—and look at sample portfolios for different life stages—in the next couple of chapters.

Why 9+ Years? The History of Market Recoveries

The **Cellar** (Long-Term Bucket) holds stocks because, historically, they are the best engine for building wealth. But that engine has a habit of backfiring. Stocks are volatile, and when they crash, they can leave a massive hole in your portfolio. To keep you from panicking and selling at the bottom, we need to know exactly how long that "hole" takes to fill back up.

How much breathing room is enough? Let me show you some of the biggest "stress tests" in American history to find the answer.

The Great Depression (1929–1932)

This was the deepest hole ever dug in the stock market. The S&P 500 effectively collapsed, losing **86%** of its value in just under three years. [68]

If you just looked at the stock price, it took 25 years to get back to "even." That sounds terrifying, but it's not the whole story. If you include the dividends (the "rent" the companies pay you) and account for the fact that prices for everything else were actually dropping (deflation), the real recovery of your **purchasing power** happened in about **8 years**. [69]

The Oil Crisis Crash (1973-1974)

This was a different kind of nightmare. Instead of prices dropping, energy costs skyrocketed and inflation went through the roof. The market took a **48%** dive.[70] It was a "twin-engine" disaster: your stocks were worth less, and your groceries cost more.

Even in this brutal environment, the total return recovery (counting dividends) happened in about six years. However, because inflation was eating away at the value of every dollar, it took a full **9.1 years** for investors to truly recover the actual buying power they held before the crash. [71]

A Tale of Two Crashes (2000–2011)

The start of the 21st century was a brutal "stress test." Investors were hit with two massive market collapses within a single decade. This era is often called the "Lost Decade," but when you look closer, it was actually a lesson in how quickly the "engine" can fix itself if you don't stall it.

The Dot-com Crash (2000-2002). When the tech bubble burst in March 2000, the S&P 500 dropped by nearly **49%**.[72] If you only looked at the stock price on the news, you would have waited seven years to see your money again. But if you were reinvesting dividends (your "rent"), you were back to even by October 2006—about 6.5 years after the peak. Even accounting for inflation, you were "whole" and in the black before the next crisis even hit.

The Great Financial Crisis (2007-2009). Just as the world was recovering, the banking and housing markets collapsed.[73] This was a deeper dive—the market fell **56%**. Yet, despite the panic, the recovery was surprisingly fast. Including dividends, investors who stayed the course reached their breakeven point by May 2011, just **3.5 years** after the crash started.

When you adjust for the actual buying power of those dollars, the recovery was complete in **4.8 years**.

The 9-Year Verdict

When we look at these three distinct eras—the deflationary 1930s, the inflationary 1970s, and the double-whammy of the 2000s—a clear pattern emerges.

While stock prices can stay depressed for what feels like an eternity, actual recoveries have historically happened much faster. By counting dividends and accounting for the changing value of the dollar, every major crash in American history reached a real breakeven point within roughly nine years.

Market Crash	Type of Crisis	Real Recovery (Total Return)
Great Depression	Deflationary	8.0 years
Oil Crisis	Inflationary	9.1 years
Dot-com Bubble	Tech Crash	7.4 years
Financial Crisis	Banking/Housing	4.8 years

Note: This is based on a century of data. While these patterns have been remarkably consistent, the past isn't a crystal ball. Future recoveries could take longer, which is why we don't just rely on history—we build safety into the "Now" and "Soon" buckets first.

The Takeaway

The 9-year rule isn't a guarantee, but it is a powerful shield. History suggests that the **Cellar** (Long-Term Bucket) needs at least a decade of breathing room. By locking the door for 9+ years, you are giving your investments the best possible chance to climb out of a

> hole, even if you happened to buy in on the worst possible day. You aren't betting on a sure thing; you are betting on the most lopsided historical odds available.

A Word of Caution: I'm an author, not your personal advisor. Everything we just discussed—the 4Qs, the buckets, and the recovery timelines—is for your education. This isn't a direct command for your brokerage account. Investing is a contact sport, and the risk of losing your money is real. Before you pull the lever on your own savings, make sure you've read the full "Universal Disclaimer" at the front of this book.

CHAPTER 9: THE BACHELOR FOUNDATION

Forget the Wall Street "Pros" with their $5,000 suits and $50 words. They use complex math to justify high fees, but our man, **Mr. Dumb Money Manager**, is here to prove them wrong.

He lives in the U.S., works a standard 9-to-5, and earns $60,000 a year. He isn't trying to outsmart the market—he's just here to out-discipline it.

The Dumb Logic: The professionals obsess over "stock picking." Mr. Dumb Money Manager focuses on what actually moves the needle: **Asset Allocation and keeping costs low**. He doesn't need a PhD to get rich; he just needs a plan he can stick to when the rest of the world is panicking.

In this chapter, we're turning the Three-Bucket Strategy into a blueprint. We're going to look at his life to illustrate the mechanics of how bucket sizes might be determined.

MR. DUMB MONEY MANAGER ENTERS THE WORKFORCE

Mr. Dumb Money Manager is 25 years old and just landed his first "real" job. His salary is $60,000 a year, which sounds like a lot of money until the government takes its cut. To build his Bachelor Foundation, he doesn't use complex spreadsheets. He uses the **50/30/20 split.** [74] It's the simplest way to divide his after-tax (net) pay without getting a headache:

- **50% for Needs:** The non-negotiables like rent, insurance, and groceries.
- **30% for Wants:** The fun stuff—dinners out, hobbies, and the latest gear.
- **20% for Savings:** The "Fuel" that he pours into his Three-Bucket Strategy.

> **DUMB NOTE:** While 20% is the "Gold Standard," treat it as your baseline. If your situation permits you to save more without living on ramen noodles, feel free to crank that number up. The more fuel you add now, the faster your **Money Machine** reaches cruising altitude.

MR. M'S FINANCIAL SNAPSHOT

Here is the cold, hard math of Mr. Dumb Money Manager's life. After Uncle Sam takes his cut and the health insurance is paid, he's left with a "Net" take-home of $4,100.

The Bucket Plan	Monthly Amount	What is included?
Needs (50%)	$2,050	Rent, groceries, and staying alive.
Wants (30%)	$1,230	Life's "little luxuries" and fun.
Savings (20%)	$820	The Fuel for the 3-Bucket Strategy

Note: For illustrative purposes only; actual results may vary and this does not constitute financial advice.

With $820 every month, Mr. M is no longer just "saving"—he's building. He isn't tossing cash into a random account and hoping for the best; he's filling his Three Buckets to handle everything from an exploded tire to his retirement.

PHASE 1: BUILDING THE SAFETY NET

TIMELINE: 15 MONTHS (THE START)

Because he is early in his career, his priority is building financial safety while capturing the "free money" from his employer's 401(k) match. Here is his sample allocation:

PHASE 1: SAFETY + GROWTH

Bucket	Asset	Monthly $	%	Why?
Short-Term (ST)	HYSA	$670	81.7%	3-month emergency fund.
Medium-Term (MT)	-	$0	0%	No medium-range goals yet.
Long-Term (LT)	S&P 500 Index Fund (401k)	$150 ($300 with match)	18.3%	Capture 100% match by contributing 3%.
Total (Excluding Match)	—	$820	100%	Excludes $150 employer match

Note: Monthly contributions only; actual balances depend on market performance and interest. HYSA stands for high yield savings account. For illustrative purposes only; actual results may vary and this does not constitute financial advice.

THE PHASE 1 MATH

- **The 3-Month Moat:** At 25, Mr. M's "sleep-well-at-night" number is three months of essentials. It's a lean, mean foundation for a single guy with no mortgage. The math is simple: (Needs + Wants) × 3 months = ($2,050 + $1,230) × 3 = $9,840.
- **401(k) Grab**: He immediately contributes 3% ($150) to his 401(k) to snatch the full company match. Never walk past free cash.
- **The 15-Month Sprint:** With $670 ($820 - $150) left for his safety net each month, hitting that $9,840 goal becomes a 15-month mission ($9,840 goal / $670 monthly savings = 14.68 months).
- **The Victory Lap**: By the time he finishes Phase 1, he'll have contributed $10,050 ($670 x 15) to his HYSA and $2,250 (15 months x $150) to his 401(k). With the employer match adding another $2,250, he reaches a total of $4,500 in new funds for his Long-Term Bucket. He's built a momentum most people his age will never see.
- **The "Checking Account" Buffer:** Before he even looks at his buckets, Mr. M keeps 1–2 months of cash in his everyday checking account. It ensures he can pay for a pizza or a power bill without having to "break the glass" on his emergency fund.

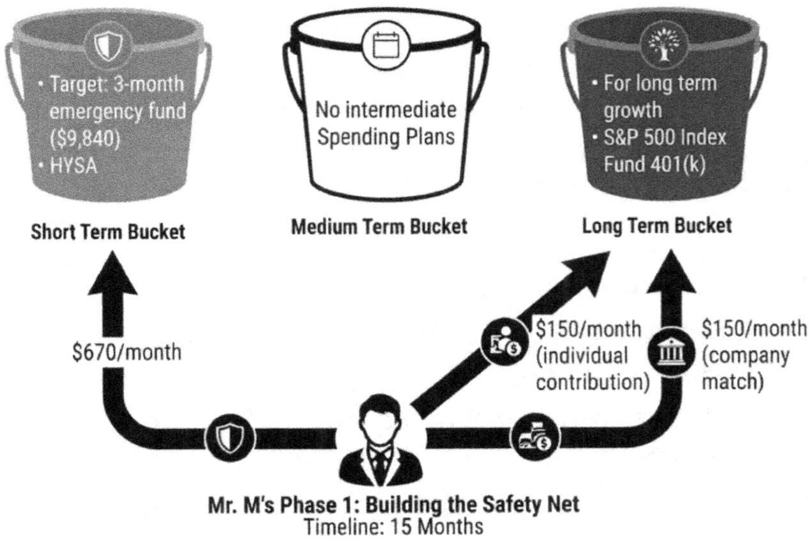

The 401(k): Your Automated Wealth Machine

The 401(k) is the most powerful tool in your financial arsenal for one reason: it automates your discipline. It's an employer-sponsored plan that lets you invest a slice of your paycheck before the tax man ever sees it.

Why it moves the needle:

- **The Invisible Tax Break:** Since contributions are "pre-tax," the IRS only taxes what's left. If you earn $5,000 and put $500 into your 401(k), you're only taxed on $4,500. You're essentially lowering your tax bill while paying your future self.
- **The Only Real "Free Lunch":** The employer match is a 100% instant return. If your boss offers a 3% match, that is a guaranteed 3% raise—but only if you show up to the table and contribute your part first.

- **"Out of Sight, Out of Mind":** Because the money is snatched before it hits your bank account, you never have the chance to blow it on a whim. This "forced" consistency is the secret sauce of every middle-class millionaire.

2026 Rules of the Road

• **Limit**: $24,500 (if you're under 50)

• **Catch-up**: $7,500 (for those aged 50–59 and 64+)

• **Withdrawal**: 59½ (standard age to avoid penalties)

• **The Penalty**: 10% plus income tax if withdrawn early.

PHASE 2: THE CAR AND THE CLIMB

TIMELINE: 2 YEARS/24 MONTHS (THE BUILD UP)

Now that Mr. M has his $10,000 "**Oxygen Tank**" sitting in his High-Yield Savings Account, he's ready to build. He isn't just surviving anymore; he's planning. He needs a car to get to work, but he also knows life is unpredictable at 25. He might move, go back to school, or switch industries.

He is sticking to his $820 monthly savings, but he's shifting the aim. He is bumping his 401(k) to 5% to push for more growth while still hoarding cash for his next big move.

PHASE 2: FLEXIBILITY + CAR GOAL + GROWTH

Bucket	Asset	Monthly $	%	Why?
ST	HYSA/ CDs	$570	69.5%	Car + Flexibility
MT	—	$0	0%	No medium-range goals.
LT	S&P 500 (401k)	$250 ($400)	30.5%	Bumping to 5% for more aggressive growth.
Total (Excluding Match)	—	$820	100%	Excludes $150 employer match

Note: Monthly contributions only; actual balances depend on market performance and interest. For illustrative purposes only; actual results may vary and this does not constitute financial advice.

THE PHASE 2 BREAKDOWN

- **The "Options" Strategy:** Because Mr. M is undecided between a car, a move, or a degree, he is stacking his extra cash into the Short-Term bucket. This isn't just saving; it's buying **options**. If his plans change in six months, he has the liquidity to pivot without breaking his foundation.
- **Squeezing the Interest:** For cash he knows he won't touch for at least a year, he can swap the HYSA for **one-year CDs**. They usually offer a slightly higher "rent" on his money.
- **The 24-Month Stash**: In 2 years, he will have contributed an extra $13,680 ($570/mo) in the Short-Term Bucket. Whether that becomes a down payment

on a car or a relocation fund, he's the one holding the cards.

- **The Long-Term Leap:** By bumping his 401(k) to 5%, he's playing the long game. Over these 24 months, he'll contribute $6,000 ($250 x 24). With his boss tossing in another $3,600 ($150 x 24), his Long-Term bucket grows by $9,600 while he's busy living his life.

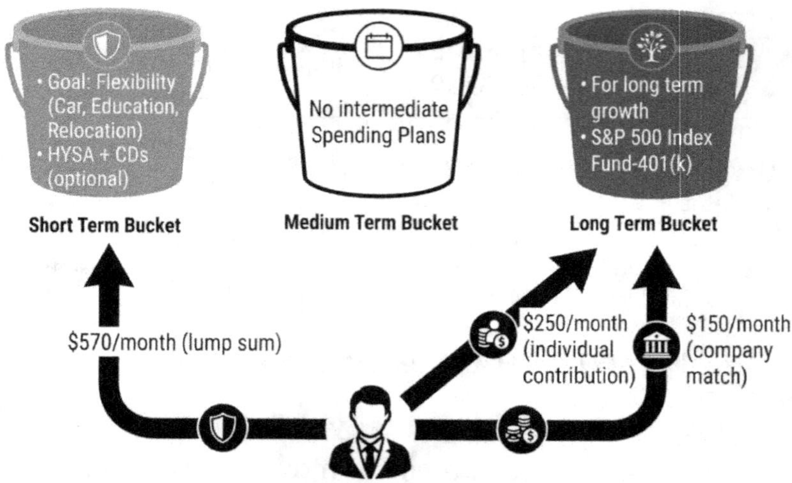

Mr. M's Phase 2: The Car and the Climb
Timeline: 2 Years/24 Months

PHASE 3: THE ROTH PIVOT & MAX GROWTH

TIMELINE: 13 MONTHS (THE STRATEGIC PIVOT)

After two years of disciplined saving, Mr. M is sitting on $13,680 in his Short-Term bucket (plus his $10,050 emergency fund). He's staying at his job, and it's time to pull the trigger on the car.

Instead of blowing the entire war chest, he puts **20% down ($5,000)** and finances the rest. This preserves his cash for a major strategic move: **The Roth Pivot.** Now that the car is in the driveway, we aren't just saving cash anymore—we're hunting for tax-free growth.

The Mission Objectives

1. **The Roth Pivot:** Re-route the surplus cash remaining in his car fund to maximize long-term growth.
2. **Adjust the Fuel:** Adjust his ongoing savings engine to account for the new car payment while keeping his long-term growth on track.

PHASE3: THE ROTH IRA PIVOT (OLD MONEY)

After cutting the $5,000 check for the car down payment, Mr. M is left with $8,680 of excess funds sitting in his Short-Term Bucket ($13,680 from Phase 2 - $5,000).

We aren't letting that cash sit around and collect dust in a standard bank account. We're putting it to work. The play here is to shift that surplus into a tax-free **Roth IRA**. But we aren't going to dump the entire $8,680 into the S&P 500 Index Fund on a random Tuesday. Instead, we use **Dollar-Cost Averaging (DCA)** to smooth out the ride.

THE MOVE-IN STRATEGY:

- **The 2026 Cap**: He'll move $625 a month from his savings into his Roth IRA. By December, he'll hit the $7,500 annual limit right on the mark.

- **The January Finish:** We've extended this phase to **13 months** specifically so he can move that final $1,180 ($8,680 - $7,500) into his 2027 bucket the second the new year kicks off. This completes the pivot and clears the board.

By deploying the money this way, he manages the risk of a sudden market dip while ensuring every dollar eventually ends up in a tax-free "stronghold" where the IRS can't touch the gains.

The Roth IRA: The Tax-Free Sanctuary

A Roth IRA is built on a simple trade: you pay the "tax man" now so you can ignore him later. Unlike a 401(k), you contribute **after-tax dollars**—money that has already been skimmed by the IRS. In exchange, every dollar of growth is yours to keep. Forever.

The Strategy:

- **The Federal Shield:** When Mr. M reaches 59½, he can withdraw his mountain of cash without owing the federal government a single cent.
- **The State Bonus:** In most corners of the U.S., the state also keeps its hands off his qualified withdrawals.
- **Universal Access:** You don't need a special employer to get one. Whether it's a major brokerage or a simple investment app, a Roth is accessible to anyone with an internet connection and a few bucks to invest.

PHASE 3: THE MAX GROWTH (NEW MONEY)

With a new car in the driveway comes a new reality: a **$375 monthly car payment**. This shifts Mr. M's investable "fuel" from $820 down to **$445** ($820 - $375).

He isn't saving less because he's lazy; he's just redirected some of his cash flow toward the car. But because his "Oxygen Tank" (emergency fund) is already full, he can now take every single remaining dollar and fire it at his Long-Term bucket.

Bucket	Asset	Monthly $	%	Why?
ST	HYSA/ CDs	$0	0%	The fortress is built.
MT	—	$0	0%	Still keeping the field clear.
LT	S&P 500® (401k)	$445 ($595)	100%	Full-throttle growth
Total (Excluding Match)	—	$445	100%	Excludes $150 employer match

Note: For illustrative purposes only; actual results may vary and this does not constitute financial advice.

THE PHASE 3: BEHIND THE NUMBERS

- **The Car Math:** We're basing that **$375 payment** on a $20,000 loan at 5% interest over 5 years. It's a solid middle-of-the-road estimate for a 2026 purchase.
- **The 13-Month Haul:** By the end of Phase 3, Mr. M has fired $5,785 of his own cash into his 401(k). When you add the $1,950 in "free money" from his employer

match, his Long-Term bucket grows by $7,735 in just over a year.

- **Room to Grow:** Even with this push, he's still well under the 2026 IRS limit of $24,500. He has plenty of "ceiling" left if he gets a raise or a bonus.
- **The Milestone:** At 29 years old, Mr. M has officially hit his stride. He's four years into his career and has a fully-funded safety net, a new car, and a tax-free growth engine firing on all cylinders.

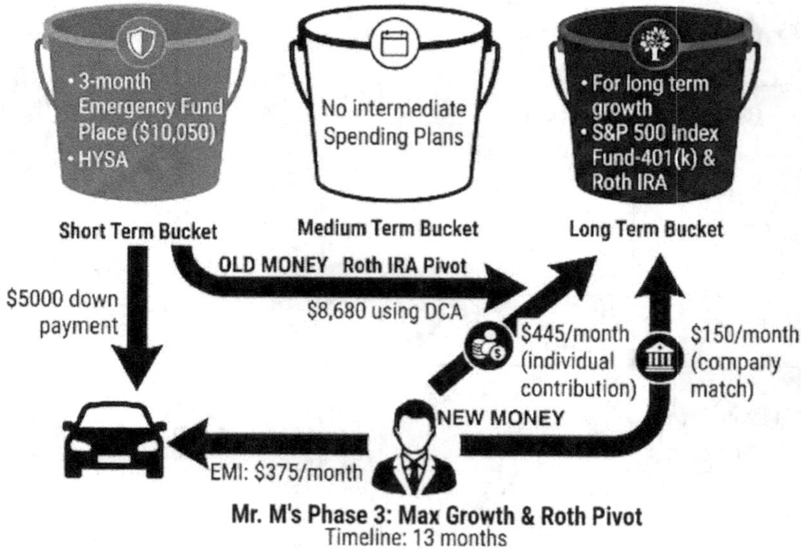

THE SCORECARD (PHASES 1-3)

Here is the full view of the board after three phases. Even with a new car in the driveway, the total wealth hasn't just stayed steady—it's gained ground.

Bucket	Short-Term (Cash)	Medium-Term (Bridge)	Long-Term (The Engine)
Phase 1: The Start	$10,050	-	$4,500
Phase 2: The Build Up	$13,680	-	$9,600
Phase 3: The Roth Pivot	-$5,000 (car) -$8,680 (Roth IRA Pivot)	-	$7,735 + $8,680 (Roth IRA Pivot)
Total	$10,050	-	$30,515

Note: For illustrative purposes only; actual results may vary and this does not constitute financial advice

BEHIND THE SCORECARD

- **The Safety Net is Untouched:** Throughout the car purchase and the pivot, Mr. M's original **$10,050 "Oxygen Tank"** remained locked and loaded. He never risked his security to buy the wheels.
- **The Contribution Reality:** These totals represent the raw cash injected into the system. In the real world, market returns and interest will likely have these numbers sitting even higher over a period of time, but we track the "**Fuel**" (contributions) to stay grounded.

LIFESTYLE VS. FOUNDATION

- **The Leak:** If Mr. M had let his spending drift upward—the classic "lifestyle creep"—the buckets wouldn't have filled. Every dollar spent on a "maybe" item was a dollar stolen from his retirement vault.
- **The Accelerator:** By being aggressive with his savings early on, he didn't just "invest"—he created a

strong footing for a house or other life goals years before his peers even started thinking about it.

THE BACHELOR LIFE WRAP-UP

We've watched Mr. M move from simply getting by to standing on firm ground. This wasn't about complex math; it was about adopting a set of habits that he can repeat for the rest of his life.

- **The 50/30/20 Filter:** This served as the "sorting hat" for his income. It provided the objective rules he needed to stop guessing and start allocating.
- **Buckets Over Ratios:** Forget the 80/20 or 70/30 stock-to-bond debates. By using the Bucket Strategy, Mr. M knew exactly what his cash was for—the "**Safety Net**" fund—and what his investments were for—the "**Retirement Vault**." Clarity beats a "target date fund" every time.
- **The Simple Engine:** He didn't win by outsmarting the market. He won by being the most disciplined person in the room—using **Dollar-Cost Averaging** into a low-cost S&P 500 index fund. He stopped trying to predict the future and started participating in it.

Let's Level Up: Mr. M is our test pilot, not a prophecy. The numbers used in this chapter are designed to show you the mechanics of the system—how the buckets flow and how the engine starts from zero. In the real world, life is messier than a spreadsheet. Your tax situation, your local cost of living, and your personal starting line will look different. Use this as a guide to understand the logic, but do the math for your own life. And as always, remember that the market doesn't take orders from anyone—check the full legal disclaimer at the front of the book before you start building.

CHAPTER 10: THE HOUSEHOLD GAME

The solo years are behind us. We've built the foundation, established the footing, and mastered the basic mechanics. Now, it's time to level up. We're fast-forwarding the timeline to the moment Mr. M becomes part of a **dual-income powerhouse.**

In the world of the Household Game, things get bigger, faster, and—if handled correctly—a lot more powerful.

THE SCOPE OF THE MISSION

We aren't here to model every possible "what if" of a forty-year life. If we tried to account for every 529 college plan, every potential inheritance, or the exact cost of diapers in 2030, the blueprint would become unreadable noise.

Instead, we're stripping away the distractions to focus on the **Big Three**:

1. **The Marriage Merge:** How two separate engines become one powerhouse.
2. **The Homeownership Pivot:** Planning for the most expensive goal on the board.
3. **The Retirement Bridge:** Ensuring the "Long-Term" engine stays ahead of inflation and life's demands.

We're keeping the model lean so the mechanics stay clear. This is about the strategic transitions that move the needle.

THE HOUSEHOLD TEAM-UP

Mr. & Mrs. M are now in their early 30s, bringing in $80,000 and $60,000 respectively. With a young child at home, they're focused on building a shared foundation while planning for their biggest milestone yet: **buying a home.** To keep the math simple, they've scaled the **50/30/20 Filter** to their joint income, sorting their combined take-home pay into three familiar lanes: Needs, Wants, and Savings.

THE JOINT SNAPSHOT: 2026 EDITION

Category	Monthly Allocation	The Game Plan
Gross Income	$11,667	Before taxes and payroll deductions
Take-Home (Net)	$8,750	What actually lands in the bank account on payday.
Needs (50%)	$4,375	The "Keep the Lights On" fund (Rent, Groceries, Childcare).
Wants (30%)	$2,625	The "Life is for Living" fund (Travel, Dining, Fun).
Savings (20%)	$1,750	The Growth Fuel. This is what we'll split across our buckets.

Note: For illustrative purposes only; actual results may vary and this does not constitute financial advice

Mrs. M didn't come to the marriage empty-handed. She brought her own stash to the table, allowing the couple to start the Household Game with a **$25,000 Safety Net**—

enough to cover three months of life if the engine stalls. They also keep a **$10,000 Cash Buffer** in their checking account to handle day-to-day "leakage." This buffer is the first line of defense, ensuring they can handle a surprise car repair or a high grocery bill without ever having to touch their **Safety Net**—or worse, dipping into their **Retirement Vault.**

However, we're also carrying some baggage from the bachelor years. Between their two cars, the couple is paying **$675 a month in EMIs** ($375 for him, $300 for her). We're operating on the reality that these payments have about three years left on the clock. It's a temporary drag on the engine, but it's one we've baked into the bucket math from day one.

PHASE 4: THE HOMEOWNERSHIP MISSION

TIMELINE: 6YEARS/72 MONTHS (THE DUAL ENGINE)

To figure out how much house they can actually handle without suffocating their other buckets, the couple leans on the **25% Take-Home Rule.** By capping their monthly housing costs at 25% of their $8,750 joint take-home income, they've set a hard ceiling of $2,188.

> **The 25% Guardrail**
>
> This is the hard ceiling: keep your total monthly housing costs—mortgage, taxes, insurance, and those

> annoying HOA fees—at or below **25% of your take-home pay**.
>
> By setting this limit, you aren't just budgeting; you are building a fortress around your lifestyle. It's the single most important move to ensure you own the home, rather than the mortgage owning you. It keeps the "Retirement Fund" growing even while you're paying off the front porch.

Of that $2,188 monthly limit, roughly **two-thirds** will tackle the **Principal and Interest** (assuming a 30-year mortgage at 6% with 20% down). The remaining **third** is swallowed by the "invisible" costs: property taxes, insurance, and those inevitable HOA fees.

This math gives us a clear target. For Mr. and Mrs. M, the "Safe Zone" for a home price is between $300,000 and $320,000. This requires a down payment of roughly $60,000 to $64,000. It's a significant number, but hitting it ensures they aren't **"house poor"** the moment they turn the key.

ACT 1: YEAR 0-3 (THE CAR DRAG)

Bucket	Asset	Monthly $	%	Why?
ST	HYSA/CDs	$0	0%	Fully Funded.
MT	Bond Fund	$608	57%	Sweet spot for growth and stability.
LT	S&P 500® (401k)	$467 ($817)	43%	4% contribution + full match
Total	—	$1,075	100 %	Excludes $350 employer match

Note: HYSA stands for high yield savings account. For illustrative purposes only; actual results may vary and this does not constitute financial advice.

ACT 2: YEAR 4-6 (THE HOME STRETCH)

Bucket	Asset	Monthly $	%	Why?
ST	HYSA/CD	$1,283	61%	Moving to cash as the goal is near (< 3 years).
MT	Bond Fund	$0	0%	Goal Met. Shifting to absolute liquidity.
LT	S&P 500 (401k)	$467 ($817)	39%	4% contribution + full match.
Total	—	$1,750	100%	Excludes $350 employer match

Note: HYSA stands for high yield savings account. For illustrative purposes only; actual results may vary and this does not constitute financial advice.

PHASE 4: THE MISSION SUMMARY

- **The 6-Year Target:** At their current pace, Mr. and Mrs. M are on track to have their full down payment ready in exactly 72 months—assuming life stays relatively stable.
- **The "Car Raise":** Over these six years, they will contribute $68,076 for their home. Notice the jump: in Year 4, that $675 monthly car payment stops being a drag and starts being fuel, nearly doubling their house-savings speed overnight.
- **The Bond Play:** We're using a high-quality intermediate bond fund for this goal. Cash (HYSA) is too slow to keep up with inflation, and long-term bonds are too risky if interest rates spike. A fund with a 5–6-year duration hits the absolute "sweet spot"—it

offers better growth than a savings account without gambling the down payment on the stock market's mood swings.

- **The Stock Alternative:** If they are willing to be flexible on Closing Day, they could put this money into the S&P 500. But fair warning: stocks are volatile. If the market dips in Year 6, they'd have to wait out the storm before getting the keys.
- **Protecting the Vault:** Even while hunting for a home, they never stop feeding the Retirement Engine. By contributing 4% each, they secure every penny of the employer match—the only 100% return they'll ever find.
- **The $58k Bonus:** By contributing 4% of their $11,667 monthly gross income—roughly $467 every month—Mr. and Mrs. M will have poured $33,624 into their 401(k)s by the end of this 72-month mission. When you add the $25,200 in "free money" from the employer match ($350 per month), they'll walk into their new home with an extra $58,824 in new funds waiting for them in the Long-Term Bucket.

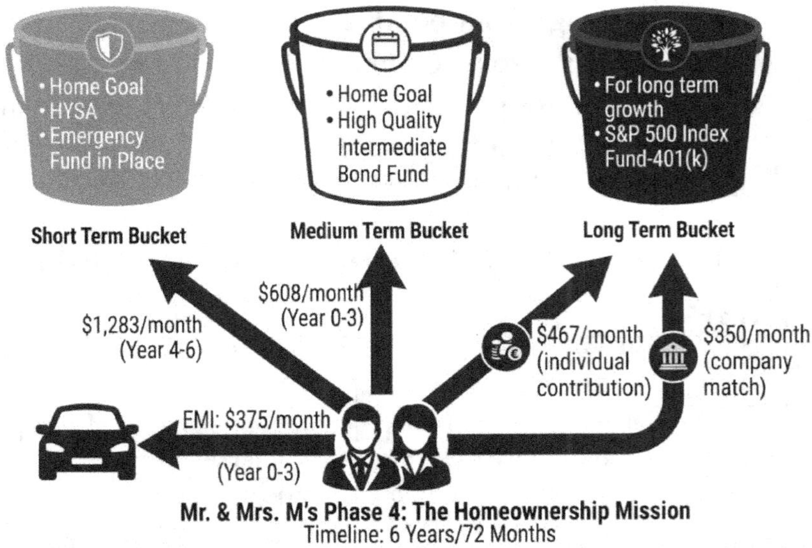

INTERMEDIATE BOND FUND: EXIT STRATEGY

As the home purchase gets closer, we don't just "hope" the bond market behaves. We need a plan to pull that money out without getting caught in a sudden interest-rate spike. Mr. and Mrs. M have two ways to handle the exit:

- **The "Sudden Stop" Move:** They could pull the entire fund in Year 4 and park it in cash. However, if the bond market happens to be down when they hit "sell," they lock in those losses, leaving less money for the down payment.
- **The Strategic Glide Path:** This is the pro move. Instead of one big exit, they **de-risk** gradually. Over the final three years, they move chunks of the bond fund into the Short-Term Bucket (HYSA/CDs). By

slowly "gliding" from bonds to cash, they shield their house stockpile from sudden market mood swings. By the time they are ready to sign the papers, the bulk of their money is sitting safely in a liquid account, protected from interest-rate drama.

THE GLIDE PATH WITHDRAWAL STRATEGY

Year	Action	Result
4	Sell 1/3 of Bond Fund → Move to HYSA	33% of the stash is now "locked in" and safe.
5	Sell another 1/3 of Bond Fund → Move to HYSA	66% is now shielded from market swings.
6	Sell the final 1/3 of Bond Fund → Move to HYSA	100% Secure. Every dollar is liquid and ready.
7	Mission Accomplished	Withdraw from the HYSA and get the keys.

Note: HYSA stands for high yield savings account. For illustrative purposes only; actual results may vary and this does not constitute financial advice.

PHASE 5: THE RETIREMENT SUPERCHARGER

TIMELINE: ABOUT 17 YEARS/204 MONTHS (THE LONG CLIMB)

Mr. and Mrs. M are now in their late 30s, and the "Household Game" has shifted. They've got the keys to the house, the car loans are a distant memory, and their earning power has hit a new gear. Mr. M now brings $98,000 to the table, and Mrs. M contributes $70,588, pushing their combined gross income to $168,588 a year.

On a monthly basis, that's $14,049 hitting the top line, leaving them with a net $9,791 to play with every single month after the tax man takes his cut.

THE NEW 50/30/20 GUARDRAILS

Instead of letting "lifestyle creep" swallow their raises, the 50/30/20 Rule remains the permanent defensive strategy. Their **$9,791 monthly net** is partitioned into three clear missions:

- **Needs ($4,896):** Because they followed the 25% take-home pay rule in Phase 4, their housing costs fit perfectly within this 50% bucket.
- **Wants ($2,937):** Their "Life" budget scales with their income, providing more room for travel without the guilt.
- **The Engine ($1,958):** This is the star of Phase 5.

SHIFTING THE FOCUS

With the "Homeownership Mission" checked off, they aren't looking for the next big purchase. Instead, they are turning the power of their 20% savings engine toward a two-track mission: the **Retirement Vault** and the **Resilience Upgrade**.

Because the house costs are already baked into their "Needs," that nearly $2,000 monthly investment is now split between thickening their defensive armor and fueling long-term growth. They are no longer saving for a specific "thing"; they are building a fortress that allows them to ignore the market's bad moods. By keeping their "Needs" capped while their income climbed, they've created a wealth-building machine that runs on autopilot, pouring surplus cash into their immediate security and future freedom at the same time.

THE RESILIENCE UPGRADE

As Mr. and Mrs. M move through their 40s and look toward 55, the stakes of the game change. In your 20s, losing a job is a speed bump; in your 50s, it can feel like a crater. Recovery times are longer, and life's "surprises"—like a major health curveball or an aging parent needing care—get significantly more expensive.

To handle this, they need to thicken their armor. The mission here is to gradually expand their **Safety Net** from a 3-month buffer to a **12-month War Chest.** This isn't just "emergency" money anymore; it's **strategic breathing room.** By having a full year of expenses tucked away, they ensure that if the engine stalls, they never have to raid the **Retirement Vault** or kill their long-term momentum. This 12-month shield protects their peace of mind as much as it protects their portfolio, making sure "inevitable surprises" are just a nuisance rather than a disaster.

PHASE 5 (GROWTH—RETIREMENT FOCUS)

Bucket	Asset	Monthly $	%	Why?
ST	HYSA /CD	$413	21%	Expanding the Safety Net to a full 12-month War Chest.
MT	Bonds	$0	0%	No intermediate goals left.

LT	S&P 500 (401k)	$1,545 ($1966)	79%	Max growth with 11% contribution.
Total	—	$1,958	100 %	Excludes $421 employer match

Note: For illustrative purposes only; actual results may vary and this does not constitute financial advice.

PHASE 5: UNDER THE HOOD

- **The $84,000 Shield:** Over these 17-year/204 months, they will stack $84,252 into their cash reserves. This isn't just an "emergency fund" anymore; it's a fortress that ensures they never have to worry about a market dip or a job change.
- **The $400k Power Move:** Over this 17-year sprint, Mr. and Mrs. M funneled 11% of their monthly gross income ($14,049) into the Long-Term Bucket, adding a staggering $401,064 in new capital ($315,180 Personal + $85,884 Match).
- **The Hidden Equity Win:** While the bank account grows, so does the house. Starting with 20% equity, every monthly "Need" payment is quietly building a secondary layer of wealth. It's the ultimate "safety net" that they'll never have to touch.
- **Leveling Up:** By the time they hit age 55, Mr. and Mrs. M's earning power reaches a combined $243,000—with Mr. M earning $139,000 and Mrs. M earning $104,000.

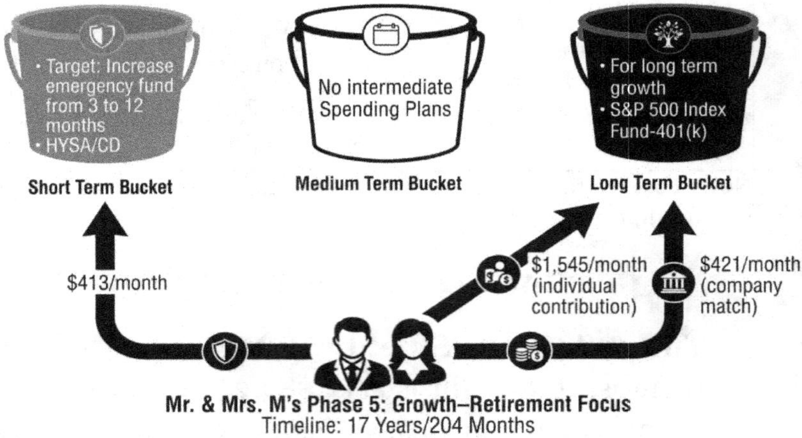

PHASE 6: THE PRE-RETIREMENT SPRINT

TIMELINE: 10 YEARS/120 MONTHS (THE FINAL ASCENT)

At age 55, Mr. and Mrs. M have officially entered the home stretch. They are at their peak earning power, bringing in a combined $243,000 gross ($20,250/month). After the tax man takes his share, they are left with a monthly net of $13,484.

They aren't taking their foot off the gas. They've adjusted their **50/30/20 Guardrails** to reflect their new reality, ensuring their "Wants" don't swallow their retirement dreams:

- **Needs ($6,742):** Covering the house, insurance, and the daily essentials.
- **Wants ($4,045):** Enjoying the fruits of their 30-year career.

- **Savings & Investments ($2,697):** The final fuel for the Retirement Vault.

With annual expenses sitting at $129,444 (monthly needs and wants multiplied by 12), the mission now is to bridge the gap between their final working day and their maximum Social Security payout.

THE RETIREMENT PLAYBOOK

Mr. and Mrs. M are eyeing a retirement age of 65 with a target lifestyle cost of $150,000 per year. To fund this, they are playing the **"Waiting Game"**—a strategy where they intentionally hold off on claiming Social Security to let the benefit grow as much as possible before they "turn on the tap."

- **The $150k Target:** Their goal is a retirement that allows for travel and comfort, which requires roughly **$12,500** in monthly cash flow.
- **The Social Security Power Move:** Instead of claiming at 65, they will wait until age 67 to lock in a **bigger slice** of the pie for life. Based on their current projections, they estimate a combined monthly paycheck of **$6,500** ($3,500 for Mr. M and $3,000 for Mrs. M).
- **Bridging the Gap:** Between ages 65 and 67, they will rely entirely on their Long-Term Bucket and **12-month War Chest** to cover their $150k annual spend. This two-year "bridge" is a strategic investment—by using their own cash early, they ensure

their government-guaranteed checks are as large as possible for the rest of their lives.

THE THREE BUCKETS REBOOT

During the earning years, the three buckets were about organizing the "Inbound" flow—balancing today's stability with tomorrow's growth. But in retirement, the mission flips. The buckets aren't just holding pens anymore; they are the **Delivery System** for your monthly paycheck.

Instead of feeding the buckets with a salary, Mr. and Mrs. M will now draw from them in a calculated sequence to create the ultimate retirement prize: **Predictable Cash Flow.**

TURNING ON THE TAP

The logic stays the same (organizing by time), but the tactics change. Here is how we put each bucket to work:

- **Short-term bucket (Years 0–3):** This is the **"Cash Tap."** It holds 3 years of living expenses in liquid, boring accounts (HYSA/CDs). This ensures that even if the stock market has a "lost year," their grocery and travel money is already locked in.
- **Medium-term bucket (Years 4–8):** This is the **"Income Bridge."** This money (typically in bonds) sits just behind the cash tap, waiting to be "promoted" to the short-term bucket as time passes. It provides a

buffer that keeps them from ever having to sell stocks during a crash.

- **Long-term bucket (Year 9+):** This remains the **"Growth Engine."** Because the first 8 years of their life are already funded by the other two buckets, this money can stay aggressive in the S&P 500, compounding quietly and replenishing the other buckets when the market is up.

SHORT-TERM BUCKET PLANNING–OUTSIDE OF 401(K)

To execute the "Waiting Game" for Social Security, Mr. and Mrs. M need a liquid launchpad. This is the **Short-Term Bucket**. Because this money must be accessible at age 65 without navigating the maze of 401(k) withdrawal rules or penalties, this bucket is built entirely with **post-tax dollars** held outside of retirement accounts.

Retirement Year	Age	Annual Expenses	Social Security	The Income Gap
1	65-66	$150,000	$0	$150,000
2	66-67	$150,000	$0	$150,000
3	67-68	$150,000	$78,000*	$72,000
Total		$450,000	$78,000	$372,000

*Assumes Social Security begins at 67.

Note: For illustrative purposes only; actual results may vary and this does not constitute financial advice.

STRATEGY NOTES

- **The $372,000 Goal:** This is the "Magic Number" for the Short-Term Bucket. It represents the total liquid cash needed to bridge the gap between their last day of work and their maximized Social Security checks.

- **The Two-Year Zero:** Notice the $0 for Social Security in Years 1 and 2. This is intentional. By living entirely on their Short-Term Bucket for 24 months, they allow their government-backed benefits to reach full-strength payout at age 67.
- **The Penalty Shield:** By keeping this **$372,000** in post-tax accounts (like an HYSA or brokerage account), the couple avoids early-withdrawal headaches and keeps their cash 100% liquid.

MEDIUM TERM BUCKET PLANNING–WITHIN 401(K)

Retirement Year	Age	Annual Expenses	Social Security	Income Gap	The Tax Adjusted Gap
4	68-69	$150,000	$78,000	$72,000	$90,000
5	69-70	$150,000	$78,000	$72,000	$90,000
6	70-71	$150,000	$78,000	$72,000	$90,000
7	71-72	$150,000	$78,000	$72,000	$90,000
8	72-73	$150,000	$78,000	$72,000	$90,000
Total		$750,000			$450,000

Note: For illustrative purposes only; actual results may vary and this does not constitute financial advice.

STRATEGY NOTES

- **The 20% Tax Buffer:** Because 401(k) withdrawals are treated as ordinary income, a **$72,000** need is actually a **$90,000** withdrawal (assuming a 20% effective tax rate). To walk away with the cash needed to fund their lifestyle, Mr. and Mrs. M must ensure this bucket holds **$450,000** by the time they retire.

- **The Social Security Floor:** Notice that the "Income Gap" stays steady at **$72,000**. This is thanks to the **$78,000** annual baseline from Social Security, which significantly reduces the pressure on their 401(k).
- **The Growth Factor:** While this money sits in the Medium-Term bucket, it isn't idle. It stays invested in bonds to stay ahead of inflation while waiting for its turn to be spent.

Based on the above calculations, Mr. and Mrs. M allocate their monthly savings and investments for ages 55–65 as follows

PHASE 6: THE SAVINGS ENGINE (AGES 55-65)

Bucket	Asset	Monthly $	%	Why?
ST	HYSA /CD	$1,250	46%	Locking in the 3-year "Cash Tap."
MT	Bond Fund (401k)	$1,447 ($2,055)	44%	Building the "Income Bridge" + 3% Match.
LT	S&P 500 (401k)	$0	0%	Let existing assets compound.
Total	—	$2,697	100%	Excludes 3% ($608) employer match

Note: HYSA stands for high yield savings account. For illustrative purposes only; actual results may vary and this does not constitute financial advice.

PHASE 6: THE STRATEGY BRIEFING

- **The $150,000 Cash Stash:** Over this 10-year sprint, Mr. and Mrs. M will pour **$150,000** ($1,250 × 120 months) into their Short-Term Bucket. When added to their existing 12-month emergency fund and a decade of compounded interest in a High-Yield Savings Account, they will have successfully bridged the "Income Gap" needed for their first three years of freedom.
- **The $246,000 Income Bridge:** Over this 10-year final sprint, the couple directed $1,447 monthly into their Medium-term bucket, adding a massive $246,600 in new capital ($173,640 Personal + $72,960 Match)
- **The Glide Path:** If the Medium-Term Bucket still has a small shortfall, it is filled using a **"Glide Path" approach.** This means gradually selling off a portion of their stock winners (Long-Term Bucket) and moving that capital into the stability of the bond fund as the retirement date approaches.

The 10-Year Glide Path: Locking in the Win

Age	Action	Rationale
55-65	Sell **$12,000** of S&P 500 Index annually (within the 401k).	Gradually tops off the Medium-Term Bucket. This creates a "safety valve" to pause sales if the market dips and resume only when prices are high.

Note: For illustrative purposes only; actual results may vary and this does not constitute financial advice.

Why this is the Ultimate Survival Tactic

By starting this pivot at age 55—a full decade before the "Retirement Launch"—Mr. and Mrs. M are building a fortress that protects them from the "What Ifs" of life:

- **The Late-Career Shield:** This decade-long build-up provides an added layer of protection against late-career risks like job loss, health issues, or unexpected home repairs. They aren't just saving for retirement; they are buying peace of mind for their 50s and 60s.
- **Crushing the "Sequence Risk":** "Sequence of Returns Risk" is just a fancy way of saying "the market crashing the day you retire." This glide path ensures that when they finally stop working, their first eight years of cash are already sitting in stable buckets.
- **The Recovery Room:** Because their short- and medium-term needs are already "bought and paid for," their Long-Term Bucket (stocks) has the breathing room it needs to recover from any market downturns without forcing them to sell at the bottom

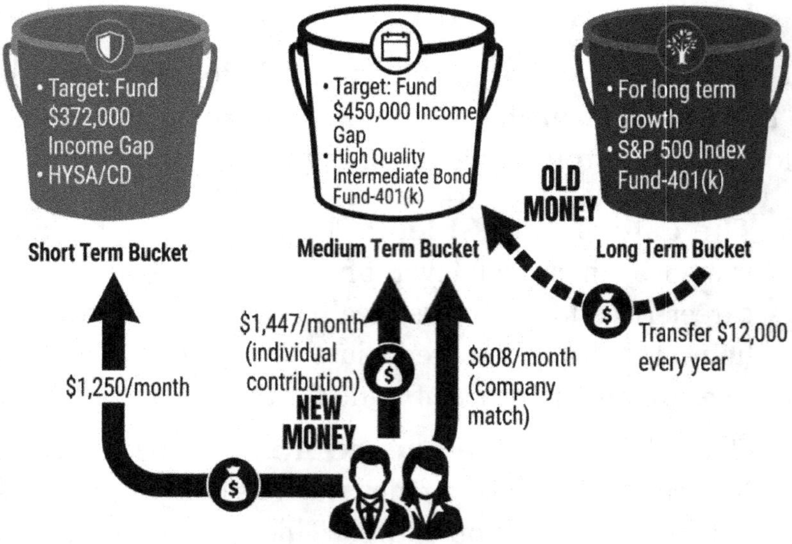

Mr. & Mrs. M's Phase 6: The Savings Engine

Timeline: 10 Years/120 Months

THE MASTER SCORECARD: (PHASE 1-6)

This is where the math meets the mission. Over the last three decades, Mr. and Mrs. M have moved from building a bachelor "Moat" to managing a high-powered joint "Engine." This scorecard tracks every dollar from Day 1 to the doorstep of retirement, showing exactly how the three buckets evolved from simple savings into a **Total Wealth Fortress**.

Bucket	Short-Term (Cash)	Medium-Term (Bridge)	Long-Term (The Engine)
Phase 1: The Start	$10,050 (Emergency Fund)	-	$4,500
Phase 2: The Build Up	$13,680 (Flexibility)	-	$9,600
Phase 3: The Roth Pivot	-$5,000 (car) -$8,680 (Roth Pivot)	-	$7,735 +$8,680 (Roth Pivot)
— Fast-Forward: Marriage & Joint Household —			
Phase 4: The Car Drag	-	$21,888 (Home Goal)	$29,412
Phase 4: The Home Stretch	$46,188 (Home Goal) + $21,888 (from MT)	-$21,888 (Glide Path to ST)	$29,412
Phase 5: The Long Climb	-$68,076 (Home Purchased) + $84,252 (Expand E.F.)	-	$401,064
Phase 6: The Final Ascent	$150,000 (Fund Income Gap)	$246,600 (Fund Income Gap)	-
Total	$244,302	$246,600	$490,403

Note: Excludes any assets Mrs. M brought into the marriage to keep things simple. E.F. stands for Emergency Fund. For illustrative purposes only; actual results may vary and this does not constitute financial advice

BEHIND THE SCORECARD

- **The Dual Engine:** The jump from Phase 3 to Phase 4 marks the moment the strategy "leveled up." By combining resources through marriage, the couple didn't just add their incomes—they accelerated their **home buying and retirement goals**.

- **The "Home" Glide Path:** Notice the $21,888 shift in Phase 4. This wasn't a random move; it was a tactical "Glide Path" to prepare for the house. By moving those funds to the Short-Term bucket early, they ensured that when the **$68,076** home purchase arrived in Phase 5, the cash was liquid and ready—leaving the "Growth Engine" completely untouched.
- **The Compounding "Iron Curtain":** While the Short and Medium-Term buckets handled the heavy lifting for the car and the home, the **Long-Term Bucket** was treated as sacred. By never raiding the 401(k) or Roth IRA for lifestyle expenses, they allowed nearly four decades of compounding to do its magic.
- **The SORR Shield:** In the final sprint (Phase 6), the focus shifted entirely to the "bridge" buckets. This wasn't about getting richer; it was about **De-Risking**. By entering retirement with their income bridge fully funded, they've built a "Sequence of Returns Risk" shield that lets them sleep through a market crash on Day 1 of retirement.

PHASE 7: THE RETIREMENT LAUNCH (WITHDRAWAL & REBALANCING)

Mr. and Mrs. M have officially crossed the finish line. On Day 1 of retirement, they aren't guessing where their next paycheck will come from—the machinery is already primed and ready. They are stepping into their new life with their **Income Gap** fully funded and their buckets positioned for the first eight years of freedom.

The Day 1 Starting Position

Before the first withdrawal is ever made, the "War Chest" is locked and loaded with the following balances:

- **The Short-Term Bucket ($372,000):** This is the liquid launchpad. Held in post-tax accounts (Cash/CDs), it is designed to cover 100% of their living expenses for the first two years and bridge the remaining gap in Year 3. Building the three-year bridge requires stacking the total living expenses for the first 24 months on top of the final Year 3 gap:

  $150,000 + $150,000 + $72,000 = $372,000

- **The Medium-Term Bucket ($450,000):** This is the "Income Bridge" held within their 401(k). It is sized to fund years four through eight. This figure includes a **20% Tax Buffer**, ensuring that even after the IRS takes its share, the couple still has the $360,000 in "spendable cash" needed to maintain their lifestyle. To build the five-year bridge, we multiply the annual income gap by the duration of the mission:

  5 x $72,000 = $360,000 (After-tax Need)

POST SOCIAL SECURITY "CRUISE CONTROL"

Once those Social Security checks start hitting the mailbox, the heavy lifting is over. The mission shifts from "bridging a gap" to **Maintenance Mode**. To keep their lifestyle secure, Mr. and Mrs. M simply need to keep the Reservoir topped off at these **recalibrated targets**:

- Short-Term Bucket (Recalibrated): Three years of Income Gap → 3 × $72,000 = $216,000
- Medium-Term Bucket (Stabilized): Five years of Income Gap → 5 × $90,000 = $450,000

THE ANNUAL REFILL: MOVING THE WATER

Once a year, Mr. and Mrs. M perform a **Tactical Reset**. They don't just spend money and hope for the best; they follow a specific sequence to ensure their Reservoirs stay full. Think of this as "re-filling the tank" after a year of driving.

They start by withdrawing their annual income gap from the Short-term bucket, then move money down the line from the "Growth Engine" to the "Tap."

Bucket	Asset	Target Value	The Tactical Action
ST	HYSA/ CD	$216,000	**The Tap:** Withdraw the $72,000 annual gap. Then, refill this bucket from the Medium-term bridge to return it to the $216,000 baseline.

MT	Bond Fund	$450,000	**The Bridge:** Once the Short-term bucket is topped off, refill this bucket from the Long-term Growth Engine (selling $90,000 of S&P 500). *
LT	S&P 500 Index Fund	—	**The Engine:** Harvest gains only when the market is "green." If the market is in a slump, we activate the **Safety Valve** and wait.

*The $90,000 refill accounts for the 20% Tax Buffer needed for 401(k) withdrawals.

Note: HYSA stands for high yield savings account. For illustrative purposes only; actual results may vary and this does not constitute financial advice.

The Strategy Debrief: Why the Reset Matters

- **The Tactical Reality:** Seeing the exact flow of $72,000 and $90,000 moves this strategy from theory into a repeatable system. It proves that even a massive income gap can be neutralized with a simple, annual reset.
- **The Longevity Shield:** By managing these 401(k) withdrawals with surgical precision, Mr. and Mrs. M ensure they never "over-spend" their reservoirs—effectively shielding themselves from outliving their money.
- **The Expense Guardrail:** Life is unpredictable, but the "Refill Sequence" provides a built-in safety check. It forces a yearly review of the "burn rate," allowing the couple to spot a high-expense year and adjust the taps before it can damage the long-term growth engine.

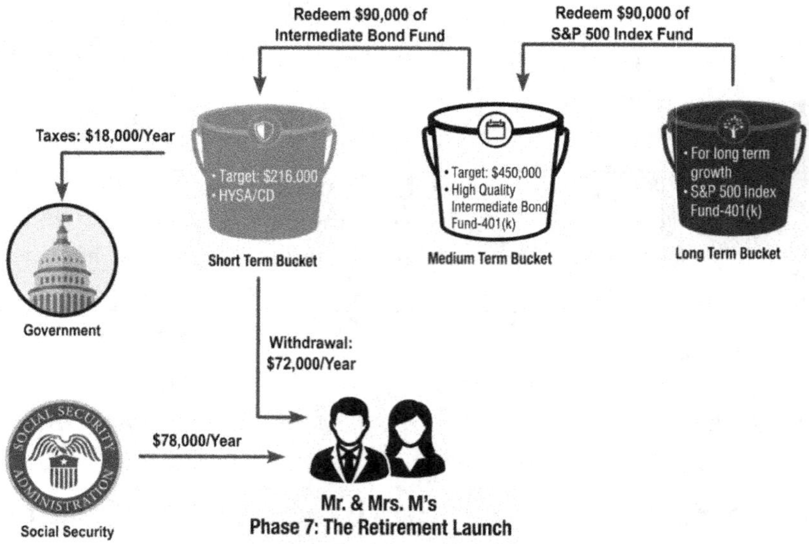

SUMMARY

The journey of Mr. and Mrs. M proves that wealth isn't about complex math—it's about **Strategic Asset Allocation.** By following the Three-Bucket Strategy, they transformed a pile of "assets" into a resilient, self-sustaining income machine.

- **The 8-Year Shield:** By securing eight years of living expenses in the Short and Medium-term buckets, the couple prioritized the **placement** of their cash over the pursuit of every last penny of growth. This created a massive safety buffer, allowing them to ignore market crashes for nearly a decade.
- **Goals over Formulas:** Instead of trusting "one-size-fits-all" formulas or Target-Date Funds that treat every investor like a number, Mr. and Mrs. M placed their

capital based on their **actual life.** This approximate, common-sense planning provides a clearer roadmap than any standardized percentage ever could.

- **Psychological Armor:** By linking every dollar to a specific timeframe—The Tap, The Bridge, or The Engine—this strategy replaces market anxiety with **Tactical Clarity.** They don't just "hope" the market goes up; they have a system where their cash is placed exactly where it needs to be, whether the market is green or red.

The Reality Check: The numbers, buckets, and strategies for Mr. and Mrs. M are built on a specific set of assumptions and historical data. While they illustrate how the **Dumb Investor** system works, they aren't a "guarantee" of what the market will do next. Your life, your tax bracket, and your risk tolerance are unique to you. Treat this chapter as a blueprint, not a prophecy. Before you make a move, do your own due diligence and check the full legal disclaimer at the start of this book.

CHAPTER 11
THE MAGIC OF COMPOUNDING AND PYSCHOLOGY OF WEALTH

In earlier chapters, we looked at how the Three-Bucket approach builds a "wall of psychological safety" around your money. By filling the **Fridge** and the **Pantry** first, you effectively ring-fence your **Cellar** (the long-term growth engine). You've isolated your future wealth from the day-to-day noise of the market and, more importantly, from the human urge to "do something" when things get shaky.

In doing so, you have secured the most valuable asset in the world of finance: **Time.**

This chapter is about what happens when you leave that Cellar door locked and let time do the heavy lifting. This is the **Magic of Compounding**—the mathematical reward for the patient, disciplined investor. To see exactly what that time is worth, let's look at the numbers.

MAGIC OF COMPOUNDING

If investing is a journey, Compounding is the engine. But an engine needs two things to get you where you're going:

Speed (your Rate of Return) and **Runway** (your Time Horizon).

THE SPEED: RATE OF RETURN

Speed determines how fast your money grows. In the early years, a 2% or 3% difference in speed feels like "pocket change." But compounding isn't a straight line; it's a curve. Because you are earning interest on your interest, a higher speed eventually causes the gap between "safe" and "growth" to explode.

THE RUNWAY: TIME HORIZON

Time is the most underrated ingredient in wealth. Compounding is "back-heavy," meaning the real magic doesn't happen in the first five or ten years—it happens in the final stretch. The **runway** needs to be long enough for the engine to hit **takeoff speed**. If you cut the journey short by panicking or raiding your accounts, you are essentially slamming on the brakes before the wheels leave the ground. You reset the clock and lose the most explosive years of "lift."

THE GROWTH OF $1,000 (BY RATE)

To see how these two drivers—Speed and Runway—actually collide, let's look at a one-time investment of **$1,000** left alone for 30 years.

Year	5% Return	7% Return	9% Return
Year 5	$1,276	$1,403	$1,539
Year 10	$1,629	$1,967	$2,367

Year	5% Return	7% Return	9% Return
Year 15	$2,079	$2,759	$3,642
Year 20	$2,653	$3,870	$5,604
Year 25	$3,386	$5,427	$8,623
Year 30	$4,322	$7,612	$13,268

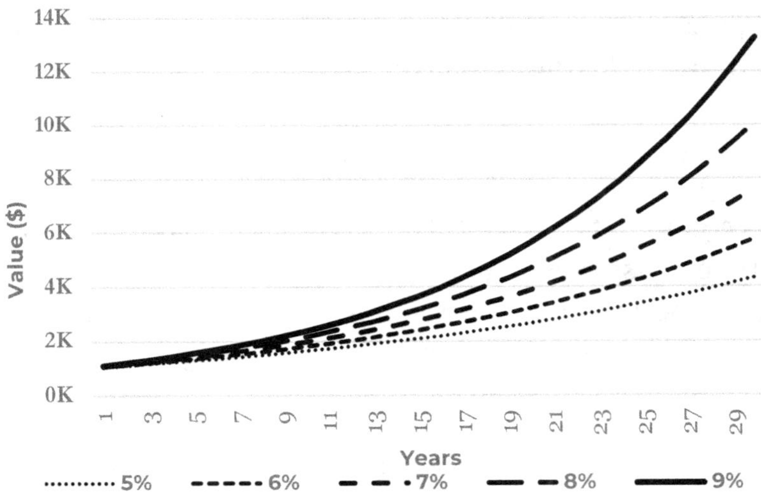

The Deceptive Early Years (0–10): Look at Year 5. The gap between a 5% and 9% return is only $263. This is the "danger zone" where many investors quit. They check their accounts, see very little progress compared to the market noise, and decide the strategy "isn't working." The magic is almost invisible in the first decade; this is the period of taxiing down the **runway**. Most people simply don't have the patience to reach **takeoff**.

The Great Crossover (10–20): By Year 20, the 9% portfolio ($5,604) is worth more than double the 5% portfolio ($2,653). This is where discipline starts to pay off. The machine is finally humming, and the gap is no longer "pocket change."

The Vertical Explosion (20–30): This is where the math gets wild. In the final five years alone, the 9% portfolio grows by $4,645. That five-year gain by itself is more than the entire 30-year value of the 5% portfolio ($4,322). This is what happens when you have enough **runway** to let the engine do its job.

THE REAL RISK OF "PLAYING IT SAFE"

It's common to avoid stocks because the market feels like a rollercoaster. For many, the "safety" of a bank account or a bond feels like the responsible choice. But while this might help you sleep better tonight, it ignores a much quieter, deadlier danger.

Staying out of the market because it feels "risky" is like refusing to fly because you're afraid of turbulence, so you decide to walk across the ocean instead. You might feel safer with your feet on the ground, but you're never going to reach the other side.

As we saw in the "Best Asset Class" chapter, equities are the high-octane fuel of your portfolio. By "**playing it safe**," you aren't actually avoiding risk—you are just trading the **risk of a market drop** for the **certainty of coming up short.** The biggest risk in investing isn't a temporary crash; it's the permanent failure to grow your money enough to actually fund your life.

DO NOT DISTURB THE ENGINE

We've seen the math: the real "magic" of compounding isn't a slow, steady climb—it's a late-stage explosion. The longer you stay on the road, the more vertical the curve becomes. But there is a catch. Because the biggest gains are packed into those final years, you have to actually make it to the end of the journey to collect them.

Every time you "tinker" with your strategy—whether you're pulling money out for a luxury, trying to "lock in profits" at the top, or panic-selling at the bottom—you aren't just taking a breather. You are cutting the power to the engine. You are resetting the clock and killing your momentum.

The Trap of "Stability"

When people say they are waiting for the market to "stabilize" before they jump back in, what they are really saying is: *"I'm waiting for the price to go much higher so I can feel safe again."* It's a trap. By the time the news feels "safe," the best buying opportunities are long gone. Trying to time the market is a fool's errand because the "perfect" entry point is a ghost—it doesn't exist. As Charles Ellis famously put it:

> **Market timing is a wicked idea. Don't try it ever... The evidence is overwhelming that most investors who try to time the market fail to even match the results of a simple "buy and hold" strategy**[75]

The Discipline of Doing Nothing

In the world of investing, the biggest winners aren't usually the smartest people in the room—they are the ones who were best at doing nothing. They didn't need to understand the "why" behind every market swing; they just had the conviction to stay in their seats while everyone else was running for the exits.

> **Do nothing.** It is the single most effective strategy for surviving the ups and downs of the market

However, this strategy only works because you own the index. If you were betting on a single company, doing nothing would be dangerous; individual companies can fail and never recover. But when you own a broad index fund, you are betting on human ingenuity as a whole. History shows that while individual players might stumble, the "team" (the market) eventually finds a way to win.

THE PSYCHOLOGY OF WEALTH

If "doing nothing" is the most effective strategy, why is it the one thing almost no one can actually do?

The reason is simple: In every other part of our lives, we are rewarded for taking action. If a pipe leaks, you fix it. If you're hungry, you find food. We are wired to solve problems by "***doing something***." But the stock market is the one place where that survival instinct is a liability. When the market drops, your brain screams at you to intervene. To survive, you have to learn how to ignore your own hard-wiring.

THE 'WORLD IS ENDING' EVENT

Market crashes aren't a bug in the system; they are a feature. We saw it in 1929, 1987, 2000, 2008, and 2020.

Every single time, the script is the same. The markets tank, headlines scream about the "end of capitalism," and your net worth starts leaking out like air from a tire. When the world around you is filled with nothing but negativity, the pressure becomes overwhelming. It doesn't just feel like a bad week; it feels like the world is ending.

In that state of fear, the logic of compounding—the "engine" we've been talking about—is replaced by a desperate urge to make the pain stop. You stop believing in the math and start believing in the doomsday. If you don't understand this psychological trap before the next dip happens, you won't just be a witness to the crash; you'll be a victim of it.

TRUST THE RECOVERY (OR BET ON THE APOCALYPSE)

The truth is simple: the market *will* crash again. Markets don't move in straight lines; they move in cycles of panic and recovery. That is a feature, not a bug.

In every previous crash—from the Great Depression to the 2008 Financial Crisis—the markets eventually recovered and reached new highs. When you realize a "dip" is just the market taking a breath before its next climb, the doomsday headlines lose their power.

Unless you believe we are witnessing the literal end of human civilization, the market will recover. We don't stay invested because we're blind to risk; we stay invested because betting against human ingenuity is a losing game. Even in our darkest hours, people still need to eat, communicate, and solve problems. The market is just a collection of those human efforts. Unless humanity is finished, the "safe" move is to trust the recovery.

YOUR BEHAVIORAL MOATS: AVOID THE PANIC

Knowing the market will crash is one thing; staying calm when it actually happens is another. To protect your compounding engine, you need more than just willpower—you need a system.

The Psychology of Wealth isn't about being "tougher" than other investors; it's about being better prepared. These strategies act as your "Psychological Insurance," ensuring that when the world feels like it's ending, you have the clarity to stay the course.

THE THREE-BUCKET MOAT

This is where your portfolio structure becomes a "behavioral moat." Most people panic because they have no barrier between their daily survival and their long-term investments. They see their money as one giant, vulnerable pile.

The Three-Bucket Strategy changes how your brain processes a crash:

Without Buckets: If the market drops **30%**, you think: *"That's my grocery money! That's my rent!"* This triggers a survival response that leads to a panic sell.

With Buckets: If the market drops **30%**, you think: *"My Long-Term bucket is taking a hit, but my life is covered for the next few years by my 'Now' and 'Soon' buckets. I don't need to touch the 'Later' engine today."* By separating your money, you buy yourself psychological time. You aren't just protecting your cash; you are protecting your ability to **do nothing** while the market recovers.

THE CHECK FREQUENCY RULE: THE POWER OF LOOKING AWAY

There is a direct correlation between how often you check your portfolio and how likely you are to make a mistake. If you check your accounts every day, you are seeing "noise"—the tiny, meaningless zig-zags that trigger anxiety. If you check once a year, you see "signal"—the long-term growth of the American economy.

Some of the people I know who navigated the 2008 financial crisis most successfully were the ones who simply never checked the impact on their retirement accounts. They didn't have "nerves of steel"; they just weren't watching the scoreboard while the game was messy. They knew they owned the whole garden, so they didn't panic when a few leaves turned brown. The rule is simple: the less you look, the better you perform. Your

Cellar is a garden, not a TV show. It doesn't grow faster because you're watching it.

SAVING FOR NO REASON

Most people only save for a specific goal, like a car or a house. But the most powerful reason to save is for **"the unknown."** Saving for no reason is your ultimate psychological insurance. It gives you "optionality"—the ability to handle a job loss, a pandemic, or a sudden opportunity without having to touch your compounding engine.

USE "LOCKED" ACCOUNTS AS A SHIELD

If your long-term money is too easy to reach, you're more likely to raid it when you get scared or want a new luxury. Using accounts like a **401(k)** or **IRA** acts as a physical and legal barrier. The taxes and penalties for early withdrawal aren't just "fees"; they are "friction" that protects your future self from your current impulses.

BE CONSERVATIVE IN YOUR PLANNING

When we look at compounding charts, it's easy to get drunk on the high-return lines. But life rarely happens at the "average." Plan your life as if the returns will be lower and the crashes will last longer. If you plan for 6% and get 9%, you're rich. If you plan for 9% and get 6%, you're in trouble. Being conservative isn't about being a pessimist; it's about building a house that can survive a hurricane.

BEHAVIOR OVER INTELLIGENCE

In the end, your net worth is a report card on your temperament, not your IQ. You don't need to be a math whiz to be a millionaire; you just need to be the person who doesn't blink when the world is panicking. A “genius” who loses their cool will always be outperformed by a “dumb investor” who knows how to stay in their seat.

A TALE OF TWO INVESTORS: THE COST OF BEING “SMART”

To see why the “Runway” (Time) matters more than the “Speed” (Money), let's look at two friends, **Early Dumb** and **Late Smart**. Both earn a 7% return, but their mindsets lead them to very different results.

- **Early Dumb:** He didn't know much about the economy. At age 25, he just started putting $1,000 a month into an index fund because someone told him it was a good idea. He did it for **10 years**, then got bored and stopped completely at age 35. He never added another cent.
- **Late Smart:** He spent his 20s “analyzing the markets.” He wanted to wait until he had a “sophisticated” strategy and a higher salary. He finally started at age 35 and, to make up for lost time, he invested $1,000 a month for the next **30 years** until he retired at 65.

The Shocking Verdict

When they both turn 65, the “Dumb” investor comes out on top.

Investor	Mindset	Total Cash In	Final Account Balance
Early Dumb	Simple & Early	$120,000	$1,413,037
Late Smart	Analytical & Late	$360,000	$1,227,087

Late Smart put in three times as much money. He worked harder, saved longer, and likely stressed more about his "strategy." Yet, he still ended up nearly **$186,000 behind**.

Why the "Smart" Guy Lost

He lost because he tried to out-think the calendar. **Early Dumb** didn't need to be a genius; he just needed to be a passenger. By the time the "Smart" guy even started his engine, the "Dumb" guy's engine was already hitting top speed. You can always earn more money, but you can never, ever buy back a missed decade.

SUMMARY: THE ENGINE AND THE EGO

Building wealth is a game of two halves: Math and Mindset. As we've seen, compounding isn't a slow, steady climb—it's a back-heavy explosion that rewards the patient. Whether you're looking at the raw power of your **Speed** (Rate of Return) or the length of your **Runway** (Time), the conclusion is the same: you cannot out-save a missed decade.

But the math only works if your ego stays out of the way. By using the Three Buckets as your psychological moat, you transform market crashes from **"world-ending"** events into mere seasonal changes. Remember the Golden Rule: the less you check the scoreboard, the better the engine runs. Your only job is to stay in your seat and let the market do the heavy lifting for you.

The Fine Print: The strategies and bucket layouts we've discussed are blueprints for how the system *can* work, not a guarantee of what the market *will* do tomorrow. Don't forget to do your own due diligence and remember: the math is there to guide you, but you are the one who has to live with the volatility. Be sure to review the full legal disclaimer at the start of this book before making any final moves.

CHAPTER 12
THE DUMB INVESTOR'S MANIFESTO

You have finished the book, but your journey is just beginning. By now, you realize that being a "Dumb Investor" isn't about a lack of intelligence—it is about a surplus of discipline. It is a refusal to play a rigged game and a commitment to a strategy that actually works.

This Manifesto is your North Star. Return to these truths not just when the world feels like it's ending, but whenever the path gets blurry:

Complexity is a trap: Wall Street sells "complicated" because they can charge for it. Simple makes you rich; complex makes them rich.

Stocks are the heavy lifters: Gold has its moments, but equities have historically won every long-distance race. Don't get distracted by shiny objects.

Short-term rollercoaster, long-term escalator: Expect the drops to turn your stomach, but trust the upward direction of the journey.

Crashes are features, not bugs: They have happened before and will surely happen again. Don't be surprised when the "World is Ending" headline return.

The "Pros" aren't winning: Most experts fail to beat a simple index fund. Stop paying for underperformance.

Market timing is a ghost: The "perfect entry" doesn't exist. Trying to find it is the fastest way to stay on the sidelines and lose momentum.

Index Funds and DCA are the answer: Buying the whole market consistently is the most powerful "Dumb" tool in your arsenal.

The Three Buckets are your behavioral moat: By separating your money by *time*, you protect your growth engine from your current impulses.

Strategy beats stock picking: Having a plan for *when* you need your money is far more important than guessing *which* stock might go up next.

The Fridge is Full: Your immediate cash is your shield. If your survival is covered, you have the power to stay calm when the market is not.

Behavior over Intelligence: Your net worth is a report card on your temperament, not your IQ.

Start early and let it run: Compounding is a late-stage explosion. The only way to win is to give it the time it needs to blow up.

A PARTING WORD

Writing this book has been a journey of its own, and I am honored that you chose to spend part of yours with me.

My goal was never to turn you into a professional trader or a math genius. My goal was to show you that wealth isn't a secret society reserved for the "experts"—it is a byproduct of simple rules, personal structure, and the courage to ignore the noise.

I hope you walk away from these pages feeling more than just educated; I hope you feel empowered. I hope the "World is Ending" headlines no longer make your heart race, and I hope you look at your three buckets with the quiet confidence of someone who finally knows where they are going.

The path of the "Dumb Investor" is simple, but it isn't always easy. While these principles are designed to be your compass, remember that everyone's map is slightly different. Before you make any major shifts or pull any levers, **always seek the counsel of a qualified financial or tax professional** to ensure your plan is tailored to your specific situation.

Go build your garden. Let the engine run. And most importantly, go live the life that your money is meant to fund.

All the best on your journey,

ANKUR BANSAL

Notes

---

1 **Board of Governors of the Federal Reserve System.** "About the Federal Reserve System." https://www.federalreserve.gov/aboutthefed/structure-and-functions.htm. Accessed December 2025.

2 **Ihrig, Jane, and Scott Wolla.** "The Fed's New Monetary Policy Tools." *Federal Reserve Bank of St. Louis.* https://www.stlouisfed.org/publications/page-one-economics/2020/08/03/the-feds-new-monetary-policy-tools. Accessed December 2025.

3 **Keynes, John Maynard.** *The General Theory of Employment, Interest and Money.* London: Macmillan, 1936.

4 **Zweig, Jason.** "Commentary on the Introduction." In *The Intelligent Investor*, Revised Edition, by Benjamin Graham, 13. New York: Harper Business, 2003. (Zweig recounts the 1720 South Sea Bubble anecdote regarding Sir Isaac Newton).

5 **Buffett, Warren E.** "Preface to the Fourth Edition." In *The Intelligent Investor*, Revised Edition, by Benjamin Graham, ix. New York: Harper Business.

6 **Bohr, Niels (Attributed).** As cited in The Art of Memory by Frances Yates (recounting a popular Danish proverb often linked to Bohr). See also: P.C.W. Davies and J. Brown, Teaching and Learning Quantum Cosmology, Cambridge University Press, 1993.

7 **Graham, Benjamin.** *The Intelligent Investor.* New York: Harper & Brothers, 1949. (This is the original text where Graham first drew his famous line between investing and gambling.)

8 **Buffett, Warren E**. "Chairman's Letter - 1996." Berkshire Hathaway Inc. https://www.berkshirehathaway.com/letters/1996.html. Accessed December 2025.

9 **Buffett, Warren E.** "Morning Session - 2019 Berkshire Hathaway Annual Meeting." CNBC Warren Buffett Archive. May 4, 2019. https://buffett.cnbc.com/video/2019/05/06/morning-session---2019-berkshire-hathaway-annual-meeting.html. Accessed December 2025.

10 **Fisher, Ken.** "You don't need perfect timing, just time, to earn big returns in the stock market." USA Today. September 16, 2018. https://www.usatoday.com/story/money/columnist/2018/09/16/stock-market-2018-avoid-timing-returns/1303307002/ Accessed December, 2025

11 **Damodaran, Aswath.** "Historical Returns on Stocks, Bonds and Bills: 1928–2024." *Stern School of Business, New York University.*

https://pages.stern.nyu.edu/~adamodar/New_Home_Page/datfile/histretSP.html. Accessed December, 2025.

[12] **Damodaran**, "Historical Returns: 1998-2024"

[13] **Buffett, Warren E.** Interview by George Goodman (Adam Smith). Adam Smith's Money World, PBS, 1985. (Often cited as the original public delivery of his "Two Rules of Investing")

[14] **Federal Reserve Bank of St. Louis.** "S&P 500 Index Total Return" and "S&P CoreLogic Case-Shiller Home Price Index." FRED. Documentation of the -80% peak-to-trough decline in equities (1929–1932) and the -27% decline in national home prices (2006–2012). Available at: https://fred.stlouisfed.org/ Accessed December, 2025.

[15] **World Gold Council** "Gold Price History." Goldhub. (2024). Data confirms significant "bear market" declines exceeding 20% in 1975 (-25%), 1981 (-32%), 1997 (-21%), and 2013 (-28%). Available at: https://www.gold.org/goldhub/data/gold-prices Accessed December 2025.

[16] **Buffett, Warren E.** Quoted in "Billionaire Talks Strategy With Students," Omaha World-Herald, January 2, 1994. (Reporting on an October 1993 lecture at Columbia University Graduate School of Business).

[17] **S&P Dow Jones.** "S&P 500 Overview." S&P Global https://spglobal.com/spdji/en/indices/equity/sp-500/#overview Accessed December, 2025

[18] **Damodaran**, "Historical Returns: 1998-2024"

[19] While 3–6 months is the standard baseline, Suze Orman suggests 8–12 months to account for longer-term economic shifts. See: CNBC, "Suze Orman explains how much money to keep in your emergency fund," June 2017. https://www.cnbc.com/2017/06/14/suze-orman-explains-how-much-money-to-keep-in-your-emergency-fund.html. Accessed December 2025.

[20] **Redfin.** "The Typical U.S. Home Changes Hands Every 12 Years, Down From 2020 Peak." *Redfin News. 2022.* https://www.redfin.com/news/homeowner-tenure-2022/. Accessed December 2025.

[21] **S&P Dow Jones Indices LLC,** "S&P CoreLogic Case-Shiller U.S. National Home Price Index (CSUSHPINSA)." Federal Reserve Bank of St. Louis (FRED). https://fred.stlouisfed.org/series/CSUSHPINSA. (Data confirms the nominal price recovery from the July 2006 peak was achieved in September 2016).

[22] **SIFMA Research**. "2025 Capital Markets Fact Book." *Securities Industry and Financial Markets Association. July 2024.* https://www.sifma.org/wp-content/uploads/2024/07/2025-SIFMA-Capital-Markets-Factbook.pdf. Accessed December 2025.

[23] **Tostevin, Paul, and Charlotte Rushton**. "How much is global real estate worth?" *Savills Impacts. October 2025.* https://impacts.savills.com/market-trends/how-much-is-global-real-estate-worth.html. Accessed December 2025

[24] **Berkshire Hathaway Inc. "2002 Annual Report."** Berkshire Hathaway, March 2003. (Letter to Shareholders, p. 15, coining the phrase "financial weapons of mass destruction"). Accessed March 2026. https://www.berkshirehathaway.com/2002ar/2002ar.pdf.

[25] **State Street Global Advisors.** "SPDR® Gold Shares (GLD®) Celebrates 20 Years." Nasdaq. November 18, 2024. https://www.nasdaq.com/press-release/spdrr-gold-shares-gldr-celebrates-20-years-state-street-global-advisors-survey. Accessed December 2025.

[26] **World Gold Trust Services, LLC**. "SPDR Gold Shares (GLD) Historical Data." *SPDR Gold Shares.* https://www.spdrgoldshares.com/usa/historical-data/. Accessed February 2026.

[27] **Federal Reserve.** "Deposit Insurance FAQs." *FDIC.* https://www.fdic.gov/resources/deposit-insurance/faq. Accessed December 2025.

[28] **Federal Reserve.** "When a Bank Fails - Facts for Depositors, Creditors, and Borrowers." *FDIC.* https://www.fdic.gov/bank-failures/borrowers-guide-fdic-insured-bank-failure. Accessed December 2025.

[29] **Federal Reserve.** "BankFind Suite: Find a Bank." *FDIC.* https://banks.data.fdic.gov/bankfind-suite/bankfind. Accessed December 2025.

[30] **S&P Dow Jones Indices LLC.** "S&P CoreLogic Case-Shiller U.S. National Home Price NSA Index [CSUSHPINSA]." Federal Reserve Bank of St. Louis (FRED). https://fred.stlouisfed.org/series/CSUSHPINSA. Accessed December 2025

[31] **Damodaran**, "Historical Returns: 1998-2024"

[32] **AMG Wealth.** "The Lost Decade, Revisited." https://wealth.amg.com/blog/the-lost-decade-revisited/; **WisdomTree**. "The Market Moves in Regimes: A Historical Look at S&P 500 Price Cycles." https://www.wisdomtree.com/investments/blog/2025/04/07/the-market-moves-in-regimes-a-historical-look-at-sp-500-price-cycles. Accessed January 2026.

[33] **Labonte, Marc.** "The Stock Market's Response to Dramatic Historical Events." Congressional Research Service.

https://www.hsdl.org/c/view?docid=47. See also: S&P Dow Jones Indices, Historical Daily Returns (Nov 1963).

34 **Investopedia.** "George Soros and Black Wednesday." *Investopedia.* https://www.investopedia.com/ask/answers/08/george-soros-bank-of-england.asp. (Referencing historical data regarding the 1992 currency crisis and the Quantum Fund's short position). Accessed December, 2025.

35 **Investopedia.** "The London Whale." *Investopedia.* https://www.investopedia.com/terms/l/london-whale.asp. (Referencing historical data regarding JPMorgan's 2012 credit derivative losses). Accessed December, 2025.

36 **Graham, Benjamin.** The Intelligent Investor. Rev. ed. New York: Harper Business Essentials, 2003. Chapter 8: "The Investor and Market Fluctuations."

37 **Graham, Benjamin.** The Intelligent Investor. 4th rev. ed. New York: Harper & Row, 1973. (See also: Buffett, Warren E. "1993 Chairman's Letter," Berkshire Hathaway Inc., where Buffett formally attributes this "voting machine" metaphor to Graham)

38 **Shiller, Robert J.** "Price Earnings Data." *Shiller Data.* http://www.shillerdata.com. Accessed December 2025.

39 **Buffett, Warren E.** Interview with CNBC's Squawk Box, February 27, 2017. See also: Berkshire Hathaway Inc. 2018 Chairman's Letter, p. 7. (Documenting the growth of the Apple Inc. position to 255 million shares at a cost of approximately $36 billion).

40 **Macrotrends.** "Apple Stock Price History: 1980–2025." *Macrotrends LLC.* https://www.macrotrends.net/stocks/charts/AAPL/apple/stock-price-history. Accessed December 2025.

41 **CNBC.** "Warren Buffett: Don't buy stocks because you think they will perform." *CNBC.* (2020). Interview with Becky Quick detailing the "yellow pad" discipline, where Buffett states that every investor should be able to write down the specific reasons for an investment before purchasing. Available at: https://www.cnbc.com/2020/02/24/warren-buffett-dont-buy-stocks-because-you-think-they-will-perform.html Accessed December, 2025.

42 **Graham, Benjamin.** *The Intelligent Investor*. Harper & Brothers. (1949). p. 28. (Graham notes that while "enthusiasm" drives innovation in art and science, in the context of security analysis, it often leads to emotional overvaluation and significant financial loss). Available at: https://www.harpercollins.com/products/the-intelligent-investor-benjamin-graham Accessed December, 2025.

43 **Investment Company Institute**. "Trends in Mutual Fund Investing, February 2025," *ICI Research.* ici.org/research/stats/trends_02_25.

44 **Investment Company Institute.** "2024 Investment Company Fact Book." *ICI.* May 2024. https://www.ici.org/system/files/2024-05/2024-factbook.pdf. Accessed December 2025.

45 **Investment Company Institute.** "2024 Investment Company Fact Book."

46 **Investment Company Institute.** "2024 Investment Company Fact Book."

47 **Nasdaq, Inc.** "Nasdaq Composite Index Overview." Nasdaq https://indexes.nasdaqomx.com/Index/Overview/COMP Accessed December, 2025

48 **S&P Dow Jones.** "Dow Jones Industrial Average Overview." S&P Global https://www.spglobal.com/spdji/en/indices/equity/dow-jones-industrial-average/#overview Accessed December, 2025

49 **S&P Dow Jones Indices.** "Exhibit 8: Percentage of U.S. Equity and International Funds Underperforming Benchmarks Each Year." SPIVA U.S. Year-End 2024 Scorecard. March 2025. https://www.spglobal.com/spdji/en/documents/spiva/spiva-us-year-end-2024.pdf. Accessed December 2025.

50 **S&P Dow Jones Indices.** "Exhibit 8: Percentage of U.S. Equity and International Funds Underperforming Benchmarks Each Year.

51 **S&P Dow Jones.** "S&P MidCap 400 Overview." S&P Global https://www.spglobal.com/spdji/en/indices/equity/sp-400/#overview Accessed December, 2025

52 **S&P Dow Jones Indices.** "Exhibit 8: Percentage of U.S. Equity and International Funds Underperforming Benchmarks Each Year.

53 **S&P Dow Jones.** "S&P SmallCap 600 Overview." S&P Global https://www.spglobal.com/spdji/en/indices/equity/sp-600/#overview Accessed December, 2025

54 **S&P Dow Jones Indices.** "Report 1a: Percentage of U.S. Equity Funds Underperforming Their Benchmarks (Based on Absolute Return)." *SPIVA U.S. Year-End 2024 Scorecard.* March 2025. https://www.spglobal.com/spdji/en/documents/spiva/spiva-us-year-end-2024.pdf. Accessed December 2025.

55 **Investopedia.** "John Bogle: Vanguard Founder and Pioneer of Index Investing." Investopedia https://www.investopedia.com/terms/j/john_bogle.asp Accessed December, 2025

56 **Bogle, John C.** The Little Book of Common Sense Investing. John Wiley & Sons, Inc., 2017.

57 **Buffett, Warren E.** "2017 Letter to Shareholders." Berkshire Hathaway Inc. https://www.berkshirehathaway.com/letters/2017ltr.pdf Accessed December, 2025

[58] **Buffett, Warren E.** "1993 Letter to Shareholders." Berkshire Hathaway Inc. https://www.berkshirehathaway.com/letters/1993.html Accessed December, 2025

[59] **Federal Reserve Bank of St. Louis.** "Market Yield on U.S. Treasury Securities at 10-Year Constant Maturity (DGS10)." *FRED Economic Data.* https://fred.stlouisfed.org/series/DGS10. Accessed December 2025.

[60] **Federal Reserve Bank of New York.** "Creditor Recovery in Lehman's Bankruptcy," *Liberty Street Economics* https://libertystreeteconomics.newyorkfed.org/2019/01/creditor-recovery-in-lehmans-bankruptcy Accessed December 2025

[61] **PBS NewsHour.** "Enron Creditors to Get 14.4 to 18.3 Cents on Dollar." *NewsHour Productions. July 2003.* https://www.pbs.org/newshour/economy/business-july-dec03-enron_07-11. Accessed December, 2025.

[62] **Damodaran.** "Historical Returns: 1928-2024," accessed December 2025. Historical reasoning synthesized from Federal Reserve Economic Data (FRED) and Investopedia market archives.

[63] **Graham, Benjamin**. The Intelligent Investor. New York: Harper & Brothers, 1949. (Note: The revised edition with commentary by Jason Zweig and preface by Warren Buffett was released in 2003).

[64] **Investopedia.** "Strategic Asset Allocation (SAA) Definition." Accessed January 2026. https://www.investopedia.com/terms/s/strategicassetallocation.asp.

[65] **Investopedia.** "Glide Path." Accessed January 2026. https://www.investopedia.com/terms/g/glide-path.asp; **Investopedia.** "Target-Date Fund (TDF)." Accessed January 2026. https://www.investopedia.com/terms/t/target-date_fund.asp.

[66] **Evensky, Harold.** "The Cash Flow Reserve Strategy." (1985); Morningstar. "The Bucket Approach to Building a Retirement Portfolio." https://www.morningstar.com/portfolios/bucket-approach-building-retirement-portfolio; **Investopedia.** "Bucket Strategy vs. Systematic Withdrawals: Knowing the Difference." https://www.investopedia.com/articles/financial-advisors/060815/comparison-bucket-strategy-vs-systematic-withdrawals.asp. Accessed January 2026.

[67] **Investopedia.** "Dollar-Cost Averaging (DCA) Definition." https://www.investopedia.com/terms/d/dollarcostaveraging.asp.

[68] **Wikipedia.** "Closing Milestones of the S&P 500." https://en.wikipedia.org/wiki/Closing_milestones_of_the_S%26P_500; **S&P Global.** "S&P 500 Through History." https://www.spglobal.com/spdji/en/documents/campaigns/sp-500-through-history-202301.pdf. Accessed January 2026.

69 **Robinson Value Management.** "The Great Impression." https://www.robinsonvalue.com/wp-content/uploads/2019/11/08Q3.pdf. Accessed January 2026.

70 **Wikipedia.** "Closing Milestones of the S&P 500." https://en.wikipedia.org/wiki/Closing_milestones_of_the_S%26P_500. Accessed January 2026.

71 **S&P Global.** "S&P 500 Through History." https://www.spglobal.com/spdji/en/documents/campaigns/sp-500-through-history-202301.pdf; Robinson Value Management. "The Great Impression." https://www.robinsonvalue.com/wp-content/uploads/2019/11/08Q3.pdf. Accessed January 2026.

72 **Investopedia.** "Dot-com Bubble." Accessed January 2026. https://www.investopedia.com/terms/d/dotcom-bubble.asp.

73 **Investopedia.** "The Great Recession." Accessed January 2026. https://www.investopedia.com/terms/g/great-recession.asp.

74 **Warren, Elizabeth and Tyagi Warren.** *All Your Worth: The Ultimate Lifetime Money Plan.* (2005); **Investopedia.** "The 50/30/20 Budget Rule Explained With Examples." https://www.investopedia.com/ask/answers/022916/what-502030-budget-rule.asp. Accessed January 2026

75 **Ellis, Charles D**. Winning the Loser's Game. New York: McGraw-Hill, 1985.

www.ingramcontent.com/pod-product-compliance
Lightning Source LLC
LaVergne TN
LVHW020234210926
848481LV00016B/1855